DIRECTIONS OF A TOWN

DIRECTIONS
OF A TOWN

A History of Harvard, Massachusetts

by Robert C. Anderson

THE HARVARD HISTORICAL SOCIETY

For Robin

Printed in the United States of America.

International Standard Book Number: 0-916782-01-8

Cover illustration by Sol Levenson, from a sketch by Walt
Harris.

Second Printing 1998

PREFACE
AND ACKNOWLEDGMENTS

When I was first approached with the idea of writing a brief history of Harvard, my first act was to find a copy of Nourse's *History of Harvard* at the library. After reading portions of his history, I realized that Nourse was very much in command of his material, and had written a town history far superior to most other such volumes. I felt, however, that his book suffered in one aspect; like so many other town historians, Nourse had organized his material topically rather than chronologically. Thus there are sections on churches, schools, military affairs, and so on.

I wanted to attempt something different—a connected, chronological narrative in which Harvard's history was treated in reasonably well-defined chunks of time, with all the institutions and events of any one chunk of time related to one another, and also related to earlier and later periods. My hope in choosing this approach was that a better picture of the development of the town as a whole would emerge. I leave it to the reader to decide whether or not I have been successful.

This organizational decision led me to select as my main source of factual information the many volumes of Harvard town records, which are remarkably complete and well-preserved. I wish to thank the Town Clerk, Helen Wood, and the rest of the ladies in her office, for their assistance and unfailing good humor in response to my repeated requests for access to the town records.

Use of the town records have made this a comprehensive history of the town, but time limitations have prevented an exhaustive investigation of all the source materials available, especially those for the last century or so. Any future historian of Harvard will find many avenues of research that have not been fully explored.

I have also received valued assistance, especially in the early stages of research, from the town clerks of Lancaster and Stow, the Massachusetts Historical Society, the New England Historic Genealogical Society, the Congregational Library, and the Massachusetts State Archives, where Leo and Helen Flaherty make research pleasurable as well as profitable.

Closer to home, I wish to thank Selectman Mario Barba for much of the original encouragement in beginning this work, and for answering many questions at all stages of the work; Nancy Case for moral support and for her work on the maps; and especially Elvira Scorgie for reading the entire manuscript and making many important corrections and suggestions based on her unsurpassed knowledge of the town's history.

Much of the geographical discussion in Chapter One derives from Neil Jorgensen's delightful book *A Guide to New England's Landscape* (Barre Publishers, Barre, Mass., 1971). Material on the early history of Lancaster and Groton was obtained from *History of the Town of Lancaster, Massachusetts* by the Rev. Abijah P. Marvin (Lancaster, 1879), *The Early Records of Lancaster, 1643–1725*, Henry S. Nourse, ed., (Lancaster, 1884), and *History of the Town of Groton* by Caleb Butler (Boston, 1848), as well as from the manuscript records of the town and from the State Archives. There is no adequate history of Stow, but material was found in the town clerk's office, and at the State Archives.

The interesting fact that the Reverend William Emerson, of Concord, father of the Reverend William Emerson of Harvard, and grandfather of Ralph Waldo Emerson, visited Harvard before the Revolution was found in *Diaries and Letters of William Emerson, 1743–1776*, arranged by Amelia Forbes Emerson, 1972, privately printed by Thomas Todd Printers, Boston.

CONTENTS

1

THE RIVER, THE BEAVER, AND THE INDIAN

About ten thousand years ago the last Ice Age ended and the glacial ice, which had reached as far south as Long Island, Martha's Vineyard, and Nantucket, began to recede. As it moved northward, the ice front revealed a landscape whose contours were not greatly different from those we see today.

When the region now occupied by Lancaster, Groton, and Harvard was freed from ice, but before the Merrimack River Valley was uncovered, a large body of water known to geologists as Lake Nashua covered much of the low-lying areas in what was to become the Nashua River Valley. Because the remaining glacial ice to the north blocked the natural flow of the water in that direction, the lake drained to the south, probably into Narragansett Bay. Some time later the ice moved far enough north to clear the Merrimack River Valley, allowing Lake Nashua to drain to the north through this new outlet. And so the Nashua River, which drains the western half of Harvard, was born. The westernmost strip of the town drains directly into the main course of the river, while the central portion of the town gives its waters to Bowers Brook, a stream that flows the length of Harvard from south to north, passing through Bare Hill Pond along the way, and emptying into Nonacoicus Brook, which turns to the west just north of the Harvard line and flows directly to the Nashua.

The freeing of the Merrimack River Valley allowed other watersheds the opportunity of disposing their waters to the north—particularly Stony Brook, one of whose tributaries is Bennett's Brook, which drains the northeast corner of Harvard; and the Concord River, which receives the waters of Assabet Brook, into which flow the waters from the corner of Harvard southeast of Oak Hill.

With the main courses of these brooks and rivers settled in their northward ways to the Merrimack, the area in and around Harvard had taken on a look that would be recognizable to us today. Though a stream or river might alter by some yards the location of its riverbed, or a portion of a hillside might be lost by erosion, on a larger scale the features were set. The glacier left as its record those characteristic physical features that will be encountered as the story of Harvard unfolds—a scattering of hills, some as high as 600 feet; Bare Hill Pond and a number of smaller ponds; the valleys, lowlands, and wetlands sheltered by the hills; and numerous streams, flowing through the valleys and feeding Stony Brook, Assabet Brook, and—the dominant feature of the town—the Nashua River.

The river, then, had taken its place. But this was a barren landscape: nothing could live under the ice, and the retreating glacier laid bare hills and valleys of churned-up gravel. Very soon a wide variety of flora and fauna moved in from the south and the land came alive. Spruce trees sprang up, and then hardwoods and other conifers. A multitude of forest-dwelling animals migrated to the newly uncovered lands in the north. Of these we should take special note of the beaver and other fur-bearing mammals that lived in and near the slow-moving streams left behind by the glaciers. The many gently sloping valleys with their streams and wetlands were made to order for the beaver, who built his dams and became one of the most important and abundant inhabitants of these freshly grown forests.

But one more element was yet to be added to the environment dominated by the river and the beaver. Not long after the withdrawal of the ice, the new inhabitants of the young woodlands were joined by yet another migrant—the North American Indian. Indian remains dating from a short time after the end of the last Ice Age are found in a number of places in New England. These were almost certainly not the same Indians that the Europeans encountered thousands of years later, but the arrival of these Indians at this early time marked the end of a relatively abrupt transition period and the beginning of ten millenia of comparatively gradual change. For with the arrival of the Indians, all the elements of a stable, balanced ecology were present. The artifacts tell us that the Indians did not remain unchanged during these ten millenia; most important, their means of gathering food changed slowly, evolving from hunting and gathering, with no domesticated plants or animals, to a somewhat more settled mode in which a few plants at least had been brought under cultivation.

In this fashion the region which would become Harvard passed a relatively peaceful ten thousand years. One tribe of Indians might be replaced by another; the oak might replace the spruce as the dominant species of tree; the main bed of the Nashua River might be displaced ten yards to the west. But no event of these ten thousand years could compare in magnitude or in abruptness with the two events which mark off this period like a pair of bookends—the end of the Ice Age and the coming of the Europeans.

At the advent of the Europeans most of the Indian tribes of New England were divisions of the Algonkians, all speaking languages which were closely related to one another, even if mutually unintelligible. The Nashua River Valley was occupied by the Nashaways, a subdivision of that group of Algonkians known as the Nipmucks. This was the northeasternmost extension of the Nipmucks, whose territory extended south into what would be northern Connecticut and west to the Connecticut River. The Nipmuck territory was bounded to the north and northeast by the Penacook tribes, and to the east by the Massachusett tribes.

The Nashaways had once been a powerful tribe, but by the

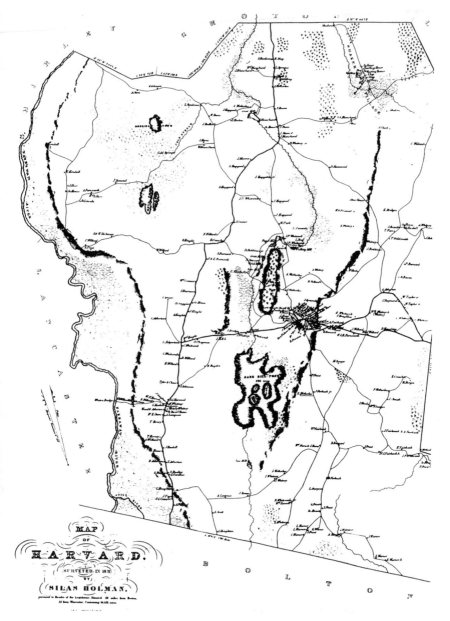

Perhaps the most beautiful map ever drawn of Harvard was Silas Holman's 1831 engraved survey, of which the above is a section. (Courtesy Albert E. Anderson)

early 1600s retained only remnants of their former strength; whether they were reduced by the wasting disease that had laid low the Massachusett tribes and others at about this time, or by some other set of circumstances, is not known. When the Europeans finally encountered the Nipmucks, these Indians were a weak and insignificant aggregation. The Nashaways, for example, paid tribute to the Penacooks to the north.

Contact between the Europeans and the Indians of northeast North America first began in the 1500s, but was infrequent and not widespread—Verrazanno at Narragansett Bay in 1524, Cartier on the St. Lawrence in the 1530s, and the largely undocumented fishermen at Newfoundland throughout the century. Meetings between the two increased in number and range in the early 1600s, as exploration and fishing, particularly by the English, grew in scale. Then in 1620 the Pilgrims came to Plymouth, the 1620s saw limited settlement of the region around Massachusetts Bay, and in 1630 the arrival of the Winthrop fleet at Salem signalled the beginning of a new era.

Until the 1630s the Europeans with few exceptions had not penetrated the interior of the New England region, and the Indians of the interior knew them only by reputation. By the mid-1630s, however, Puritan settlement had begun to move away from the coast, largely for economic reasons. Agricultural surpluses and a merchant fleet had not yet been developed, and the economy of the infant Massachusetts Bay Colony was heavily dependent on the export of beaver and other mammalian furs to England to pay for the imports of food and other scarce necessities.

With this incentive Concord was established in 1635 and Sudbury in 1639. The leading spirit in the settlement of Concord was Simon Willard, a trader and adventurer who had learned of the presence of beavers in the wetlands of the Musketaquid (or Concord) River Valley; part of this information he probably obtained from the Indians of that area. Simon Willard headed a group of men who obtained a patent for a new township, which they immediately settled, making this the most isolated plantation in the Bay Colony at that time. The town flourished from its very beginning.

The glacier had left behind the landscape, dominated by the river; the river and the valley had attracted the beaver and the Indian; when the Puritans first settled New England, they needed beaver pelts, which they obtained by trade with the Indians.

The river, the beaver, and the Indian—these provide the background for the establishment of the Puritan towns which gave birth, decades later, to the town of Harvard.

§ Bare Hill and Bowers Brook

In its many occurrences in the early records of Lancaster and Harvard, the name of this local elevation is consistently spelled "Bare Hill," and is not seen as "Bear Hill" until well into the eighteenth century.

The name Bare Hill stems from a practice of the New England Indians of annually burning the underbrush in the forests. This left the heavily wooded hills easily passable to a man on horseback. The early settlers of Lancaster were apparently impressed especially by the openness on the 600-foot hill in the northeast part of the town, and bestowed upon it the name Bare Hill.

The stream that runs north from the Harvard-Bolton line, through Bare Hill Pond, and on toward Ayer is now known as Bowers Brook. But in early records the portion of the brook north of Bare Hill Pond was called Brook Meadow Brook, and some of the wetlands along the way were known as Brook Meadow. Further north, as other streams joined Brook Meadow Brook, the name changed to Nonacoicus Brook, and that name has been retained for the stream in Ayer on its way to the Nashua River. Sometime after the incorporation of Harvard, the Bowers family moved into town and built a mill on the brook south of Bare Hill Pond. This part of the stream became known as Bowers Brook; in time, this name was extended to what had earlier been Brook Meadow Brook.

2

LANCASTER, GROTON, AND STOW

Eight years after the establishment of Concord, a similar venture was begun in the Nashua River Valley, but the circumstances were somewhat different. In 1643 Sholan, the sachem of the Nashaways, came down to the Bay and offered to sell some of his land in return for the establishment of a trading post in his territory. Sholan's motive may have been simply to obtain some of the prized European trade goods, or perhaps he wanted to ally himself with the powerful Puritans in order to free his tribe from the domination of the Penacooks; but whatever his purpose, his desire was fulfilled, for in that same year Thomas King of Watertown set up a trading post on the eastern slope of George Hill, not far from Nashaway, the confluence of the north and south branches of the Nashua River. With the Nashaway Indians supplying King with beaver skins from the various streams that fed the Nashua River, the fragile foundations of a new plantation were laid.

Thomas King was not long associated with the outpost at Nashaway; a group of traders headed by John Prescott acquired the trading franchise in 1644, and the plantation grew steadily throughout the 1640s. Before 1652 the fledgling settlement initiated the series of petitions that would eventually lead to incorporation in 1653 and acquisition of full township privileges in 1654. The town, now known as Lancaster, experienced some difficulties in self-government, and in 1657 the General Court— the legislative body of the Massachusetts Bay province— appointed three commissioners to supervise town affairs. One of these commissioners was Simon Willard, the founder of Concord and one of the leading citizens of the Bay Colony; in 1659 the townsmen of Lancaster persuaded Willard to settle in their town and not long after granted him an extensive tract of land, known as the Still River Farm, on the east bank of the Nashua.

In 1655 a second plantation was begun in the Nashua River Valley, for in that year two groups of petitioners—one from Concord, and one headed by Deane Winthrop, son of the late Governor John Winthrop—asked the General Court for permission to settle a town in the hitherto vacant land north of Lancaster along the Nashua River. These petitions were amalgamated and that same year the township of Groton was granted, only a year after Lancaster's incorporation.

During the 1650s Lancaster was a firmly established town with about thirty-five families resident, including a minister, the Reverend Joseph Rowlandson, who came in 1654. There was a grist mill, built by John Prescott. Groton during the same period led a precarious life, with no more than half a dozen families actually occupying the land granted to them. Relations between the two towns must have been amicable and frequent, for in 1658 provision was made by Lancaster for cutting a road to "the plum-trees and Grotten." (The Plum Tree Meadows were the lowlands on the east bank of the Nashua, bounded on the north by the Lancaster line and on the east by Makemachekamuck [Prospect] Hill; these meadows provided easy access to Groton's land to the north.) The two townships of Lancaster and Groton were much larger than the towns of today. Lancaster was roughly a rectangle eight miles east and west by ten miles north and south, while Groton approximated a square eight miles on a side. The two towns were not contiguous; a strip of unincorporated land about three-quarters of a mile wide ran between them.

In 1659 the Lancaster boundaries were surveyed for the first time, and in that year was made the second division of meadows, mostly in the northeast corner of the town on land that would later be Harvard or Bolton. These second division grants were made for the most part in the Still River and the Plum Tree Meadows, both on the east bank of the Nashua, and in the Pin Hill and Bare Hill Meadows, both across the hills to the east, in the valley drained by Bowers Brook and Bare Hill Pond. By 1659, and probably considerably earlier, that part of Lancaster that was to become a part of Harvard was well known to the townsmen of Lancaster and was probably to some extent in agricultural use. But the records show no residences on these second division lands at this time, and probably none were built until well after King Philip's War. In these early days of Lancaster the dwelling houses were concentrated on the neck between the north branch and the main course of the Nashua (modern Lancaster Village), and to the south in the area east of George Hill, south of the north branch of the Nashua, and west of the south branch of the Nashua (modern South Lancaster and Clinton). The meetinghouse was centrally located adjacent to the burial ground on the south bank of the north branch, near the wading place leading to the Neck.

Groton's woes were partially solved by a reorganization in 1661 and 1662, after which the population increased considerably and the town attained a more stable existence. In the next few years two attempts were made by Groton men to erect a mill for the town's use, but both failed. Finally, the town turned to John Prescott of Lancaster, a miller of proven abilities; Prescott came to terms with the Groton men, and in 1667 he and his son Jonas built a grist mill near the southern boundary of Groton on Bowers Brook. This is the first building known to have been built on Harvard soil, and the only one before King Philip's War; the site was near the mill pond south of Old Mill Road.

By the end of the 1660s, then, Puritan civilization had a strong foothold in the Nashua River Valley and neighboring regions. Lancaster and Groton were flourishing frontier towns with excellent prospects. Like Concord in the 1630s, they had passed through the period of dependence on the beaver, and were rapidly becoming settled agricultural villages with well-

Paul Revere's engraving of King Philip.

organized churches and town governments. And in 1670 a new group of men, many from Concord, petitioned the General Court for some of the land that had been left in common; the incorporation of the towns of Groton, Nashoba [Littleton], Concord, Sudbury, Marlborough, and Lancaster had formed a nearly closed ring around a tract of unoccupied land which bore the Indian name of Pompositicut. The petition was granted and a plantation begun; but this settlement, which would later become Stow, was not incorporated as a town until thirteen years later.

Life in the Nashua River Valley was rudely disrupted in 1675 with the outbreak of the bloody war with the Indian chieftain King Philip. In the following year Groton and Lancaster were abandoned to the Indians, with virtually all buildings destroyed by fire; obviously, the infant plantation at Pompositicut also suffered from the conflagration. The region remained uninhabited for the next few years, the first attempts at resettlement coming in 1679 or 1680.

This resettlement was not, however, simply a reconstruction of the devastated towns along old and familiar lines. In Lancaster the distribution of population shifted considerably eastward; many returning inhabitants took up residence on their second division lands east of the Nashua, leaving their former homesteads on the Neck or near George Hill unoccupied. In Groton the Prescotts moved their milling operation eastward to Stony Brook, although the original mill appears to have come through the war undamaged. The land formerly belonging to the mill was sold to Matthias Farnsworth of Groton, and was distributed to his sons upon his death in 1689. Some of Farnsworth's sons built homes on the lots near the old mill, and other Groton townspeople were attracted to this part of town. Consequently the southern part of Groton became more densely populated than before the war. Efforts toward the building of the plantation at Pompositicut were resumed, and in 1683 this tract of land was incorporated as the town of Stow. The strip of land between Groton and Lancaster, previously ungranted, was included within the bounds of the township and became known as Stow Leg. Grants of land were soon made in Stow Leg, but settlement did not occur until the 1720s.

King Philip's War had weakened permanently the strength of the southern New England Indian tribes. The Nashaways no longer existed as an independent tribe; the survivors of the war were absorbed into other tribes, principally the Penacooks to the north. For another three decades, though, the settlers of the valley were exposed to occasional raids by Indians still living in the wastelands to the west. Fear of such raids was probably one of the principal motives which led many Lancaster townsmen to resettle on the east bank of the Nashua, for the intervening river provided some additional protection, and homesteads on the western flanks of the hills had excellent prospects westward across the valley, affording in some cases advance warning of approaching Indians.

Additional protection was obtained through the institution of garrison houses. In each little region of settlement (each

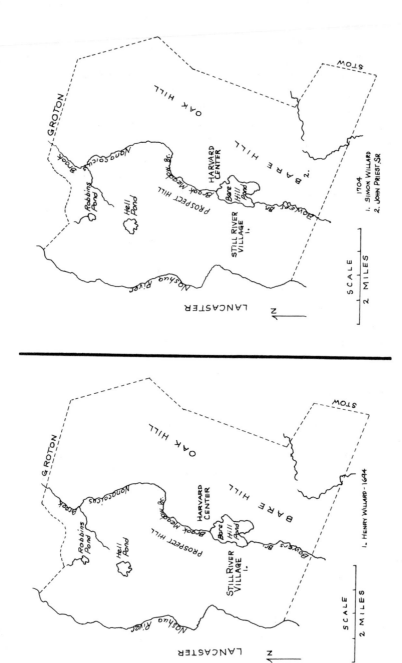

Above two maps show garrison houses in sparsely populated Harvard of 1694 and 1704.

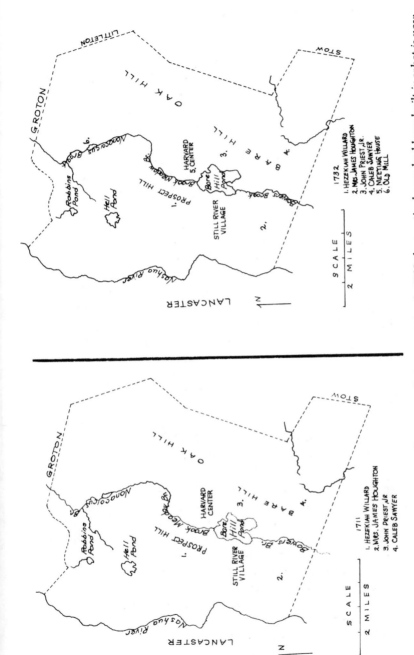

By 1711 there were four garrison houses, and by Harvard's incorporation in 1732 the meetinghouse had been built in what is now Harvard center.

neighborhood, one might say) one dwelling was designated as a garrison house; this building would be constructed of especially stout materials, with a view toward use on defensive situations. To this house a number of families would repair in times of danger for protection and mutual support. By studying lists of garrison houses much may be learned about the distribution and growth of population in these towns, particularly Lancaster.

A list of 1692 gives details of the nine garrisons in Lancaster; one of these, assigned to Henry Willard, was located on Harvard soil. Henry Willard had inherited his father Simon's land at Still River, and the garrison was undoubtedly on this land. Three other families, as well as a number of soldiers, were included in this garrison—those of Joshua Atherton, John Priest, and John Warner. Thus, less than 10 percent of Lancaster's population had moved into future Harvard territory: two families (Willard and Atherton) in Still River, and two families (Priest and Warner) on Bare Hill.

The next garrison list that has survived is dated 1704, and shows eleven garrisons in Lancaster, two of them in the Harvard region. The garrison headed by Simon Willard, son of the pioneer, and Benjamin Bellows was the successor to the Henry Willard garrison and was also located in Still River. The second garrison, headed by John Priest, senior, was designated the Bare Hill garrison. Twenty-two families were protected by these two strongholds—over 20 percent of the families in Lancaster. This expansion of population had probably occurred along an east-west axis just north of the present Harvard-Bolton line; the far northeast corner of Lancaster remained sparsely populated.

This portrait of the garrisons in 1704 is of especial interest, since it is contemporaneous with the first dispute over the location of the meetinghouse. Such arguments played a crucial role in the founding of new towns throughout colonial New England, as a reading of petitions from many towns makes clear. Once large numbers of townspeople had to journey more than three miles to the meetinghouse on Sabbath-day, dissatisfaction would follow. Attempts would be made to relocate the meeting-house, ending frequently in the establishment of two or more distinct towns—new units politically and religiously—where there had been one before. That is the path events followed in Lancaster, and the first hints of the break came in 1704.

When Lancaster was being rebuilt in the 1680s, the second meetinghouse was erected on the site of the first; the second meetinghouse was burned during an Indian raid in the summer of 1704, making necessary the construction of a third. As has been shown above, the population distribution in Lancaster had not remained unchanged during the twenty-year lifetime of the second meetinghouse. Furthermore, a similar phenomenon to that at Still River and Bare Hill was also taking place at Wataquadock, the region just to the south that gave birth to the town of Bolton. In 1705, at the time of the debates about building the third meetinghouse, the residents on the east bank of the Nashua constituted over 40 percent of Lancaster's voting strength; when they were joined by the men from the Neck, they were a majority, and could dictate the location of the new point of assembly. In 1706 the third meetinghouse was built on the east bank of the Nashua, just across from the lower end of the Neck.

Redistribution of the town's populace continued, as evidenced by the 1711 garrison list. Four of Lancaster's eighteen garrisons, representing nearly a quarter of the town's population, were located in Harvard territory. The Houghton garrison was the successor of the Simon Willard–Benjamin Bellows garrison at the lower end of the Still River settlement, and the John Priest garrison was now headed by Caleb Sawyer. The two completely new locations were the Hezekiah Willard garrison at the southern end of Prospect Hill, and the John Priest, Jr., garrison on the northern slopes of Bare Hill. The latter was the closest garrison to what would become the center of Harvard, then almost completely unpopulated. This new realignment of population had moved along two north–south axes, with expansion northward along the low hills between the main courses of the Nashua and the Bowers Brook watershed (the axis defined by the Houghton–Hezekiah Willard garrisons), and parallel to that, expansion northward along Bare Hill and the highlands to the east of Bowers Brook and Bare Hill Pond (the Caleb Sawyer–John Priest, Jr., axis).

The internal shift in Lancaster's population is reflected also in the apportionment of the schoolmaster's time, for by the mid-1720s he was teaching almost exactly half the year away from Lancaster Center, at the Wataquadock and the Still River–Bare Hill schoolhouses. The population of Lancaster in 1711 has been estimated at about 400 to 500, with one fourth of this number in the Still River–Bare Hill area. Over the next two decades, the population of the town doubled, approaching 1,000, and the population in the Still River–Bare Hill area was probably in excess of 200.

This discussion of the period after King Philip's War has focused, thus far, only on Lancaster. Groton and Stow, it appears from the records, experienced little difficulty as the result of complaints from the sections of those towns that later became a part of Harvard—Stow Leg and the southeast part of Groton. Probably, these sectors were simply considered small and unimportant relative to the entire towns of which they were parts. In Groton the principal source of discontent was the northwest quadrant—the section that would later become the town of Pepperell—where again people found it difficult to reach the meetinghouse. In this context the complaints of only nine or ten families in the southeast portion would be considered relatively insignificant, and would not have received much attention. The situation in Stow was similar. A petition of 1730 shows that the inhabitants of Stow Leg were about one-seventh of the town's total population; the problems of this minority, arising largely out of their peculiar geographical situation, would be of little interest to the majority of the townsmen. Contrast this to the arrangement in Lancaster, where one half the town on the east bank of the Nashua was opposed to the other half on the west bank; here the complaints could not be minimized or ignored.

The dissidents of the above-mentioned portions of Groton and Stow may not have made as great an impression as did their counterparts in Lancaster, but by the mid-1720s the inhabitants of these three adjacent regions (northeast Lancaster, Stow Leg, and southeast Groton) did share a number of problems and attitudes. First, all three sections were relatively new offshoots of towns whose histories went back to the period before King Philip's War. Second, and corollary to the above characteristic, all three sections were inconveniently placed with respect to the meetinghouses in the older portions of the towns, and considered this inconvenience a major grievance. Last, all three sections shared in a problem common to this entire region—the population explosion that followed the cessation of the hostilities with the French and Indians in 1713.

Out of this community of interests arose a community of action, and the residents of these outlying portions of the towns of Lancaster, Groton, and Stow soon began to think of themselves as a community in all respects. The inevitable consequence was the formation of the town of Harvard.

§ Mary Rowlandson's Captivity

The following account of the destruction of Lancaster during King Philip's War was written by Mary Rowlandson, wife of that town's first minister. She and her children were captured by the Indians; she was eventually ransomed for the sum of twenty pounds. The book she subsequently wrote about her experiences was first published in 1682 and became enormously popular. The excerpts used here are from an edition of 1856, A Narrative of the Captivity, Sufferings, and Removes of Mrs. Mary Rowlandson, *published by the Massachusetts Sabbath School Society.*

On the 10th of February, 1675, came the Indians with great numbers upon Lancaster [Mass.]: their first coming was about sun-rising; hearing the noise of some guns, we looked out; several houses were burning, and the smoke ascending to heaven. There were five persons taken in one house, the father and mother, and a suckling child they knocked on the head, the other two they took and carried away alive. There were two others, who being out of their garrison upon occasion, were set upon; one was knocked on the head, the other escaped. Another there was who running along was shot and wounded, and fell down; he begged of them his life, promising them money (as they told me) but they would not hearken to him, but knocked him on the head, stript him naked, and split open his bowels. Another seeing many of the Indians about his barn, ventured and went out, but was quickly shot down. There were three others belonging to the same garrison who were killed; the Indians getting up upon the roof of the barn, had advantage to shoot down upon them over their fortification. Thus these murtherous wretches went on burning and destroying all before them.

At length they came and beset our house, and quickly it was the dolefulest day that ever mine eyes saw. The house stood upon the edge of a hill; some of the Indians got behind the hill, others into the barn, and others behind any thing that would shelter them; from all which places they shot against the house, so that the bullets seemed to fly like hail, and quickly they wounded one man among us, then another, and then a third. About two hours (according to my observation in that amazing time) they had been about the house before they prevailed to fire it, (which they did with flax and hemp, which they brought out of the barn, and there being no defence about the house, only two flankers at two opposite corners, and one of them not finished) they fired it once, and one ventured out and quenched it, but they quickly fired it again, and that took. Now is the dreadful hour come, that I have often heard of (in time of the war, as it was the case of others) but now mine eyes see it. Some in our house were fighting for their lives, others wallowing in blood, the house on fire over our heads, and the bloody heathen ready to knock us on the head if we stirred out. Now might we hear mothers and children crying out for themselves and one another, "Lord, what shall we do!" Then I took my children (and one of my sisters her's) to go forth and leave the house: but as soon as we came to the door, and appeared, the Indians shot so thick, that the bullets rattled against the house, as if one had taken a handful of stones and threw them, so that we were forced to give back. We had six stout dogs belonging to our garrison, but none of them would stir, though at another time, if an Indian had come to the door, they were ready to fly upon him and tear him down. The Lord hereby would make us the more to acknowledge his hand, and to see that our help is always in him. But out we must go, the fire increasing, and coming along behind us roaring, and the Indians gaping before us with their guns, spears, and hatchets to devour us. No sooner were we out of the house but my brother-in-law (being before wounded in defending the house, in or near the throat) fell down dead, whereat the Indians scornfully shouted and hallooed, and were presently upon him, stripped off his cloaths. The bullets flying thick, one went through my side, and the same (as would seem), through the bowels and hand of my poor child in my

arms. One of my elder sister's children (named William) had then his leg broke, which the Indians perceiving, they knocked him on the head. Thus were we butchered by those merciless heathens, standing amazed, with the blood running down to our heels. . . . The Indians laid hold of us, pulling me one way, and the children another, and said, "Come, go along with us." I told them they would kill me: they answered, if I were willing to go along with them, they would not hurt me. . . .

I had often before this said that if the Indians should come, I should chuse rather to be killed by them, than taken alive: but when it came to the trial, my mind changed; their glittering weapons so daunted my spirit, that I chose rather to go along with those (as I may say) ravenous bears, than that moment to end my days. . . .

Now away we must go with those barbarous creatures, with our bodies wounded and bleeding and our hearts no less than our bodies. About a mile we went that night, up upon a hill within sight of the town, where we intended to lodge. There was hard by a vacant house, (deserted by the English before, for fear of the Indians). I asked them whether I might not lodge in the house that night? to which they answered, What, will you love Englishmen still? This was the dolefulest night that ever my eyes saw. Oh the roaring, and singing, and dancing, and yelling of those black creatures in the night, which made the place a lively resemblance of hell. And miserable was the waste that was there made, of horses, cattle, sheep, swine, calves, lambs, roasting pigs and fowls (which they had plundered in the town) some roasting, some lying and burning, and some boiling, to feed our merciless enemies, who were joyful enough, though we were disconsolate. . . .

The morning being come, they prepared to go on their way, one of the Indians got upon a horse, and they sat me up behind him, with my poor sick babe in my lap. A very wearisome tedious day I had of it; what with my own wound, and my child being so exceeding sick, and in a lamentable condition with her wound, it may easily be judged what a poor feeble condition we were in, there being not the least crumb of refreshing that came within either of our mouths from Wednesday night to Saturday night, except only a little cold water. . . . I sat much alone with my poor wounded child in my lap, which moaned night and day, having nothing to revive the body, or cheer the spirits of her; but instead of that one Indian would come and tell me one hour, your master will knock your child on the head, and then a second and then a third, your master will quickly knock your child on the head.

This was all the comfort I had from them; miserable comforters were they all. Thus nine days I sat upon my knees, with my babe in my lap, till my flesh was raw again. My child being even ready to depart this sorrowful world, they bid me carry it out to another wigwam; (I suppose because they would not be troubled with such spectacles;) whither I went with a very heavy heart, and down I sat with the picture of death in my lap. About two hours in the night, my sweet babe like a lamb departed this life, on Feb. 18, 1675, it being about six years and five months old. It was nine days from the first wounding in this miserable condition, without any refreshing of one nature or another, except a little cold water. I cannot but take notice, how at another time I could not bear to be in a room where a dead person was, but now the case is changed; I must and could lie down with my dead babe all the night after. I have thought since, of the wonderful goodness of God to me, in preserving me so in the use of my reason and senses, in that distressed time, that I did not use wicked and violent means to end my own miserable life. . . . God having taken away this dear child, I went to see my daughter Mary, who was at the same Indian town, at a wigwam not very far off, though we had little liberty or opportunity to see one another; she was about ten years old, and taken from the door at first by a praying Indian, and afterwards sold for a gun. When I came in sight she would fall a weeping, at which they were provoked, and would not let me come near her, but bid me be gone; which was a heart-cutting word to me. I had one child dead, another in the wilderness, I knew not where, the third they would not let me come near to . . . . [A]s I was going up and down mourning and lamenting my condition, my son came to me and asked me how I did? I had not seen him before, since the destruction of the town; and I knew not where he was, till I was informed by himself that he was amongst a smaller parcel of Indians, whose place was about six miles off. With tears in his eyes he asked me whether his sister Sarah was dead? and told me he had seen his sister Mary; and prayed me, that I would not be troubled in reference to himself. . . .

*   *   *

A Squaw was boiling horses feet, she cut me off a piece, and gave one of the English children a piece also. Being very hungry, I had quickly eat up mine; but the child could not bite it, it was so tough and sinewy, but lay sucking, gnawing and slobbering of it in the mouth and hand, then I took it of the child, and eat it myself, and savory it was to my taste. That I may say as *Job, Chap. 6. 7. The things that my soul refuseth to touch, are as my sorrowful meat.* Thus the Lord made that pleasant and refreshing, which another time would have been an abomination. Then I went home to my mistress's wigwam, and they told me I disgraced my master with begging, and if I did so any more, they would knock me on the head. I told them they had as good do that, as starve me to death. . . .

. . . [T]he Saggamores met to consult about the captives, and called me to them, to enquire how much my husband would give to redeem me. When I came I sat down among them, as I was wont to do, as their manner is. Then they bid me stand up, and said, they were the general court. They bid me speak what I thought he would give. Now knowing that all that we had was destroyed by the Indians, I was in great strait. I thought if I should speak of but little, it would be slighted, and hinder the matter; if of a great sum, I knew not where it would be procured; yet at a venture, I said twenty pounds, yet desired them to take less; but they would not hear of that, but sent that message to Boston, that for twenty pounds I should be redeemed. . . .

. . . So I took my leave of them, and in coming along, my heart melted into tears, more than all the while I was with them, and I was almost swallowed up with the thoughts that ever I should go home again. About the sun's going down, Mr. Hoar, myself, and the two Indians, came to Lancaster, and a solemn sight it was to me. There I had lived many comfortable years among my relations and neighbours: and now not one Christian to be seen, or one house left standing. We went on to a farm house that was yet standing, where we lay all night; and a comfortable lodging we had, though nothing but straw to lie on. The Lord preserved us in safety that night, and raised us up again in the morning, and carried us along, that before noon we came to Concord.

Now was I full of joy, and yet not without sorrow: joy, to see such a lovely sight, so many Christians together, and some of them my neighbours. There I met with my brother, and my brother-in-law, who asked me if I knew where his wife was? poor heart! he had helped to bury her, and knew it not; she being shot down by the house, was partly burnt, so that those who were at Boston at the desolation of the town, came back afterward and buried the dead, did not know her. Yet I was not without sorrow, to think how many were looking and longing, and my own children among the rest, to enjoy that deliverance that I had now received; and I did not know whether ever I should see them again. Being recruited with food and raiment, we went to Boston that day, where I met with my dear husband; but the thoughts of our dear children, one being dead, and the other we could not tell where, abated our comfort in each other.

3
"THE HOUSE WE NOW MEET AT FOR THE PUBLICK WORSHIP"

Our earliest evidence that a new town was in the making comes from the record of a Lancaster town meeting of January 23, 1727 —a meeting concerned largely with the subject of a new meetinghouse. Two mutually exclusive propositions were before the townspeople: Should the Lancastrians enlarge the meetinghouse then in existence, on the east bank of the Nashua? Or should two new meetinghouses be erected, presumably one for the newer settlements on the east bank and one for the older inhabitants on the Neck and just south of the Neck? A committee was asked to formulate a recommendation for resolving this issue, and in February the committee reported, suggesting that the existing meetinghouse be enlarged.

This solution was obviously only a temporary one, for enlarging the meetinghouse corrected only half the problem; the enlargement would accommodate the increase in population of the twenty years between 1706 and 1726, but did nothing to alleviate the inconveniences experienced by the increasing number of townspeople who lived at great distances from the meetinghouse.

Four years passed, during which time the inhabitants of Stow Leg, southeastern Groton, and northeastern Lancaster pooled their interests and abilities towards the solution of their common problems. What they produced was a fully-developed and well-orchestrated scheme for the detachment of these three regions from their parent towns, to be followed by amalgamation into a new political and religious entity, a new town as yet unnamed.

By the spring of 1730 the plan had ripened, and the petitioners presented their requests to the three towns involved. Groton and Stow considered the proposition at their town meetings in March 1730; the former was quite willing to accede to the wishes of the petitioners, the latter was totally opposed. Lancaster placed the question of its answer to this petition on the warrant for a meeting in May 1730. We do not know what was decided at this meeting, but from later actions of the town it may be inferred that it, like Stow, rejected the petition at this early stage. The records of the Groton meeting and the Lancaster warrant indicate that the petitioners asked for all of the southern part of Groton and the northern part of Lancaster, both east and west of the Nashua, and presumably for all of Stow Leg as well.

Apparently, the petitioners were sufficiently encouraged, at least by the response of Groton, that they then sent their request to the General Court, where it was read on July 2, 1730. The General Court notified the towns that the matter was before it, which set off another round of town meetings in August. The petition was identified as being presented by Simon Stone, Jr., Jonathan Whitney, and Thomas Wheeler. Stone lived in the old mill region of Groton, Whitney in Lancaster, and Wheeler in Stow Leg; thus each of the three towns had one representative on the committee of principal petitioners. Lancaster on August 7, 1730 voted to oppose the petition and instructed the town's representative to the General Court accordingly. Groton reconsidered its earlier vote, but only as it affected the total amount of land to be taken; the town voted on August 17 to allow the petition as it related to land east of the Nashua, but chose not to relinquish any land west of the river. Stow decided on August 20 to oppose the petition, and by the first Monday in September a committee appointed by the town had drafted a counter-petition —bemoaning the town's poverty in land and warning of the damage that would be done to the town if the petition were granted, claiming that it would be losing one-seventh of its inhabitants and even more of its agriculturally productive land.

After this second series of responses, even less encouraging than the responses of the spring meetings, the Governor's Council (at that time the upper house of the General Court) dismissed the petition, but the House of Representatives chose to keep the petition alive, and appointed a committee to investigate the matter further.

The August meetings must have told the petitioners much, for they redrafted their proposal, reducing their demands considerably. On October 9, 1730 the General Court took under consideration the new petition, and the three towns were duly notified. The three principals of the July petition were joined by Jonas Houghton of Wataquadock; the memorialists asked for all the land east of the river that they had previously requested, but this time asked for much less on the west bank, running their new line one mile west of the river, rather than at the far western bounds of Lancaster, Groton, and Stow.

As we might expect, this set off yet a third round of town meetings in November, the three towns responding much as they had in August. At this point in the proceedings the regular alternation of petition by the group of hopeful secessionists followed by response in town meeting was broken off, and a new series of petitions was begun by a variety of interested groups. Some sought to be added to the original group of petitioners; some asked that they be allowed to remain with the old portion of town; and at least one offered a counter-proposal, the acceptance of which would have made the Jonas Houghton–Simon Stone–Jonathan Whitney–Thomas Wheeler petition irrelevant. This was a petition of Jacob Houghton, cousin of Jonas, on behalf of himself and others on the east bank of the Nashua, in that part of Lancaster which is now Bolton, requesting that the old town of Lancaster be split down the middle on a north–south line to form two new towns. No mention was made of Groton or Stow; in fact this proposal appears to be a resurrection and expansion of the 1727 plan for building two meetinghouses.

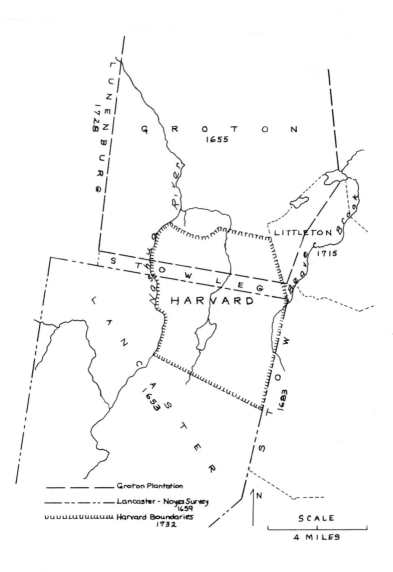

Harvard's boundaries at its incorporation in 1732.

The House of Representatives temporarily ignored this new group of requests and in December 1730 appointed a new committee. The committee was charged with investigating the Jonas Houghton petition; it was to render an opinion no later than June of the following year.

In March 1731 Jacob Houghton presented yet another petition to the town of Lancaster, asking that the section of Lancaster east of the Nashua and five miles south of the town's north boundary be constituted a new town. This was a smaller area than that requested in the first Jacob Houghton petition, but still more than the Lancaster–Groton–Stow Leg coalition had asked of Lancaster. The town this time agreed to the division of the lands of the old town and the creation of a new township in the northeast quarter; this must have been encouraging to all those petitioners who wanted to take a part of Lancaster, even if they did not agree with the Jacob Houghton plan.

This Jacob Houghton petition of March, and a dissenting petition of the same month, were also taken under consideration by the House committee, which in due course submitted its report. The report was accepted and passed by the Governor's Council on June 21 and by the House of Representatives on June 22, 1731. The document itself has not survived, but we may surmise that the issue was settled by allowing the petition of Jonas Houghton and the Lancaster–Groton–Stow Leg coalition and disallowing all others, for nothing further is heard on the subject until the following June, when the act incorporating Harvard along the lines of the Jonas Houghton plan was expeditiously carried through the legislative process. The full record of that proceeding in June 1732 follows:

Anno Regni Regis Georgii Secundi Quinto & Sexto.

An Act for erecting a New Town within the county of Worcester, by the name of [Harvard].

Whereas the Inhabitants of the extream parts of the Towns of Lancaster, Groton and Stow have laboured under much difficulty and inconvenience by reason of their remoteness from the places of publick Worship in the Towns to which they respectively belong, & have supported the Cost and Charge of preaching among them for several years past without any Consideration from their Towns, and have addressed this Court for Relief, & that they may be set off a distinct township by themselves.

Be it therefore Enacted by His Excellency the Governour, Council and Representatives in General Court assembled & by the authority of the same that the Land in the extream parts of the Towns of Lancaster, Groton and Stow as the same are hereafter bounded and described be and hereby are set off, & Constituted a seperate & distinct Township by the name of [Harvard] vizt. beginning at the Southerly End of the Causeway, near the House of Samuel Wilson in Lancaster and from thence running North West and by West till the line meets with Lancaster River, & from said Causeway running South East & by East to Lancaster East bounds then running Northerly in the East Bounds of Lancaster till it comes to Beaver Brook, then bounding on said Brook till it comes to Littleton Bounds, and then running on said Littleton line near to the Northwest corner thereof vizt. so far as that a West North West Line shall leave the dwelling house of James Stone in Groton six perch to the Northward, and continuing the same Course to Lancaster River aforesaid, excepting Coyacus Farm or so much thereof as shall fall within the bounds above said; and to bound West on said River and that the Inhabitants of the said lands as before bounded and described be and hereby are vested with all the powers privileges and immunities which the Inhabitants of any Town in this province are or by Law ought to be vested with.

provided that the Freeholders and other Inhabitants of the said Town Settle a learned and Orthodox Minister among them within the space of two years and also erect an House for the publick Worship of God.

and Be it further Enacted by the Authority aforesaid that the aforesaid Town of [Harvard] be and hereby is Declared to be within the County of Worcester, Any Law Usage or Custom to the contrary notwithstanding.

1732 June 20th. This Bill having been read three several times in the House of Representatives passed to be Enacted

1732 June 21st   J. QUINCY *Spkr*

1732 June 29 This Bill having been read three several Times in Council passed to be Enacted   J WILLARD *Secry.*

By His Excellency the Governor.

June 29, 1732. I consent to the Enacting of this Bill

J. BELCHER

Tradition has it that the name "Harvard" came about not by decision of its residents, but by the choice of Josiah Willard, then secretary to the province of Massachusetts Bay. Grandson of Major Simon Willard, and son of Samuel Willard, who was for some years president of Harvard College, Josiah was himself Harvard educated. It was probably because the secretary had many close relatives in the new town—six Willard families, all cousins to Josiah, are represented on the petition of 1730—that when Governor Belcher received the bill of incorporation with the place for a name left blank, he offered the choice to Josiah Willard, whose college loyalties prevailed.

With the signing of this act on June 29, 1732 by Governor Belcher, the town of Harvard was legally established, but various hints in the documents leading up to the incorporation imply that "Harvard" had been a functioning community for at least two years prior to the incorporation, and perhaps for even longer. The Lancaster town meeting warrant for May 17, 1730 includes the statement that inhabitants of part of Stow and Groton "have agreed and Covenanted with the petitioners" of Lancaster to ask that they be allowed to form a new town. This language implies that these groups of men from three towns had already discussed their plans in detail, come to some sort of agreement, and perhaps even drawn up and subscribed to a binding covenant, much as the early settlers of New England had done when establishing a new church or a new town. The opening paragraph of the act of incorporation itself may be interpreted to mean that the petitioners had already constituted themselves into an informal church, probably hiring preachers on a Sabbath-by-Sabbath basis. The first town meeting held at Harvard in July 1732 was assembled at "the house we now meet at for the Publick Worship," indicating that this building had been in existence for some time, perhaps from the time of the 1730 petition or earlier. These scraps of evidence—the "covenant" of 1730, the support of preaching mentioned in the act of incorporation, the church which predated the formal existence of the town—are tantalizing hints that tell much about a few dozen families who conceived of themselves as a community and acted on their conception, even in advance of their recognition by the General Court and other more formal bodies.

The location of this first meetinghouse shows clearly the willingness of the Lancastrian majority of the petitioners to accommodate the smaller numbers joining them from Groton and Stow. This house of public worship was located just north of the present Common, and at the time of incorporation most of the Lancastrian petitioners lived some distance to the south, in Still River and on the opposite slopes of Bare Hill. The Stow and Groton petitioners, of course, resided some distance to the north of this meetinghouse. The important aspect is that the meeting-house, while not near any concentration of dwellings, was convenient to all the groups that had covenanted to form the new town; this carefully chosen location obviously reflects the dissatisfaction these men and women had felt because of the inconvenient location of their old meetinghouses, and their desire to avoid the same dissatisfaction in their new community.

Just as the 1732 act of incorporation did not begin the period of transition leading to an independent, full-fledged community, neither did it bring that period to a close. Embedded in the act was a set of requirements that the newly established town must fulfill, failing which the act would be void. The townspeople of Harvard had two years in which to "settle a learned and orthodox minister among them . . . and also erect an house for the publick worship of God." These requirements were a normal clause in other acts of town incorporation in the Massachusetts Bay Province, but were not always fulfilled, since the General Court did not take much notice of laxity. The earliest records of the town of Harvard show, however, that its people took their directions quite seriously.

The first meeting of the new town was held on July 11, 1732; the only business was the election of town officers, from selectmen and town clerk to hogreeves and field-drivers. The second meeting was held on July 25, and for the next eighteen months almost every item of town business concerned either the settlement of a minister or the erection of a meetinghouse. The main concern of this second meeting was the appointment of a

Harvard's first meetinghouse, rendered using incomplete town records and information about other meetinghouses of the same period. (Drawing by Sol Levenson)

committee to supply the pulpit from week to week, a procedure that would be continued until a minister was settled and ordained in the town. The next meeting was held on August 29, at which time an attempt was made to short-circuit the problem of erecting a new meetinghouse; it was proposed instead that "the house we now meet at for the Publick Worship" be purchased by the town. This expedient measure was voted down, which left the alternative of building a new structure, a process that took another year.

The first try at settling a minister came at the meeting of September 19 when the town agreed to "give Mr. Philemon Robbins a call to the pastoral office." Mr. Robbins was a 1729 graduate of Harvard College who had not yet been called to any congregation; he may have been the minister who preached to these same townsmen before the town's incorporation. At this same meeting the town formally voted to erect a new meeting-house, and a committee was chosen to oversee the work. The town gave this committee detailed instructions about the dimensions of the building and the procedure to use in construction, and directed the committee to raise the house (presumably the frame only) no later than the first of June, 1733.

At the meeting of December 4, 1732 Mr. Robbins gave his answer to the town, refusing the call, probably because he had received a similar offer from the congregation at Branford, Connecticut, where he settled a short time later. The committee that had previously been appointed to hire a minister was instructed to continue its efforts. At the end of the meeting a committee was chosen to deal with the Lancaster proprietors about obtaining a tract of land "known as Meeting House Plain"; this proposal was received favorably by the Lancaster proprietors, and in the spring of 1733 the town of Harvard was granted about 30 acres, the remains of which form the present Common. This little transaction reminds us that although the act of incorporation had given the Harvard townsmen governmental jurisdiction over their territory, all the land not previously granted to individuals remained in the hands of the proprietors of Lancaster, Groton, and Stow to dispose of as they deemed best.

Preparations for erecting the meetinghouse continued through the early months of 1733, and Mr. Robbins was still on hand to preach, but only until a replacement could be found. On the first page of the Congregational church records Mr. John Seccomb writes: "March 11, 1733 I began to preach at Harvard upon Probation." On April 26 the town met and voted unanimously to give Mr. Seccomb, a 1728 Harvard graduate, a call to the ministry. Mr. Seccomb replied somewhat ambiguously and at great length that he appreciated the offer, but was somewhat worried that the terms of his settlement did not include provisions for increasing his salary in times of inflation or as the town prospered. The townsmen were mildly annoyed by this response, but agreed to take these circumstances into account; and on May 22 Mr. Seccomb agreed to accept the call to the Harvard ministry.

A committee was chosen at the June 13 town meeting to consult with Mr. Seccomb about the details of his ordination; and in the church records for June 20 we find that "The Meetinghouse was raised for Publick Worship." Most of the public actions of the town in the summer of 1733 revolved around the interrelated problems of ironing out the details of the Reverend Mr. Seccomb's ordination and putting the finishing touches on the newly raised meetinghouse.

Mr. Seccomb's ordination took place on October 10 with the ministers of Groton, Lancaster, Stow, and Medford (Mr. Seccomb's birthplace) participating in the ceremonies. This event no doubt witnessed the first public use of the meetinghouse, for the town records show that the town meeting of September 25 was called to order in "the House where we now meet for the Publick Worship," whereas the very next town meeting, on December 18, was held at "the Meeting-House."

In this last meeting of 1733, and in one or two meetings in 1734, the townsmen cleared up the business of building a meetinghouse and settling a minister; final reports were heard and settlements were made on bills for expenses incurred in these pursuits.

Thus by the end of 1733, only eighteen months after incorporation, the town had successfully completed the task set out by the General Court, and was assured of a secure place alongside the other established towns of the province. The close of 1733 marked the termination of a transition period. What had begun in the late 1720s as the idea of a few men in the far corners of three adjacent towns had now come to fruition. The result— the new political, religious, and social unit that would be Harvard—was, by the beginning of 1734, free to take up the continuing tasks common to all New England towns.

§ The Character of the People

Henry S. Nourse was the first to set down the annals of the town in a book; his History of the Town of Harvard, Massachusetts 1732–1893 *was published by Warren Hapgood in 1894. In it, Nourse makes the following observations on the "character of the people":*

The colonists who brought to New England their heritage of Saxon virtues and energies, did not leave behind them all the ancestral vices or passions. Though a simple-hearted folk, leading lives of loving domesticity, these grandsires of ours and their good-wives, it must be confessed, lacked refinement. They would have ill suited their environment had they not been of stronger individuality, ruder tastes, more callous natures, and every way of coarser fibre than their descendants in the fifth generation. They unblushingly "called a spade a spade." When hot with irritation they used a very vulgar vernacular. Gross lapses from moral rectitude were regularly made the subject of oral confession in the presence of the congregated church, and duly recorded by the pastor. Moreover, we are told that the self-accusations of the low-voiced, stammering sinners always won a rapt attention such as no pulpit eloquence could gain. This unsavory charge obtains force when we read in the ministers' records, that so late as 1798, "the pastor then submitted to the consideration of the brethren the propriety of abolishing the custom of making confession for the sin of fornication in *particular*," and that the proposition stirred up a "warm debate," but effected no change in the musty by-laws.

Superstitions which now seem strange then held the majority in firm bondage. During 1720, the fantastic tricks of three young girls in Littleton, who pretended to be sufferers from sorcery, caused intense excitement not only in that town but throughout the neighboring villages. Though not attended with any of that frenzy which thirty years earlier had led to wholesale murder, the sensation brought out the fact that a belief in the existence and power of witches was as rife as ever. Throughout that century and even to within the memory of the living, from time to time in Harvard individuals otherwise sober-minded have declared themselves the victims of witchcraft; usually charging their mishaps to the evil eye or magic arts of some forlorn old crone. For instance, the later years of Moses Tyler and Daniel Willard, it is said, were greatly embittered by their believing themselves afflicted by witches; and good dame Knight, when she had ill success in butter-making, never blamed her own lack of skill, but inveighed against her neighbor Goody Pollard for bewitching the cream. She declared that she one day struck with the peel a great, black spider which ran out from the churn, but, though seriously crippled, it got away up the chimney; and the next day she found out that it was a witch she had hurt, and who it was, for Goody Pollard had to send for the doctor, having been badly lamed, as she alleged, by falling down stairs. . . .

Some grim ghosts walk in Harvard tradition, mostly of undoubted kin to that of Cock Lane. The hobgoblin that made the most noise in town was that of a murdered drummer. The tale of this disturber of Harvard's rural quietude was given the author by Reverend John B. Willard: One winter's evening soon after the close of the war for independence, a traveler, weary with tramping through the deep snow, halted for the night at the Saunderson Tavern on the Littleton road. It was soon known to the landlord and the bibulous frequenters of his bar-room that the wayfarer's name was Hill, that he had served as a drummer in the patriot army, and was returning home from Boston with the accumulated wages for his service in his pocket. After that night the stranger was never again seen alive, and there is little doubt that he was killed for his money. Popular opinion pointed to a shady character by the name of McDaniell as the murderer, and the guilty connivance of the tavern-keeper was suspected. Nothing tangible was found to incriminate any one, but Saunderson soon removed from town.

Several years later, a ploughman on the farm of Ebenezer Bridge, not far from the site of the tavern, turned up a human skeleton with his furrow. The mysterious disappearance of the drummer was recalled, and the bones brought to light were at once declared to be Hill's. His father was notified of the ghastly discovery, but being too infirm to journey to Harvard, sent word that if the remains were those of his son, they could be identified by a noticeable peculiarity of the teeth. Examination of the exhumed skull disclosed the specified singularity. The bones were reburied under a tree near by.

While the affair was fresh in the minds of the people, several individuals with ears like those of Huckleberry Finn, alert for "that kind of sound that a ghost makes when it wants to tell about something that is on its mind and can't make itself understood, and so can't rest easy in its grave," asserted that they had heard the beating of a drum at night in the neighborhood of Hill's last resting place. No one claimed to have seen the wraith of the murdered man, but sober citizens who travelled the Littleton road by night began to tell of the ghostly drumming to be heard on Oak Hill. At last a hard headed and unimaginative man was found plucky enough to trace the sound to its source, and lo! the complaining ghost was but a loose splinter of a fence rail, upon which the breezes played as with an Aeolian harp string. Its fickle music in the hush of night had an uncanny tone, and human fancies and fears translated it into the muffled roll of a kettle-drum.

§ Jonas Houghton, Surveyor

Jonas Houghton was one of the most important men in the proceedings leading to the incorporation of Harvard, but he was never a resident of the town. He was born on September 2, 1682, son of Jonas Houghton and grandson of John Houghton, one of the earliest settlers of Lancaster. He learned the skills of an "artist," as surveyors were then called. Surveyors were very much in demand at that time, for with the abatement of the Indian menace in certain parts of Massachusetts and New Hampshire, families by the dozen were pulling up stakes and moving into the previously unoccupied lands on the frontier, and these lands had to be carved up into towns, and the towns into houselots and farms.

Jonas Houghton was evidently a very good surveyor, for he participated in the mapping and subdividing of a number of towns in Massachusetts and New Hampshire. Part of his compensation for his labors in each town was a parcel of land, perhaps 150 or 200 acres. In some cases he was admitted as a proprietor of the new town, and could therefore expect to receive more property in later divisions of common lands. At his death, Jonas left to his sons tracts of land in half a dozen newly established New England towns. He was especially interested in the settlement of Sturbridge, and had helped to provide land for the church. He may have intended to move there, but he died in 1739, at the age of 56, before being able to do so.

Houghton, a resident of Wataquadock (Bolton), had bought a parcel of land in Stow Leg in 1729, but does not seem to have taken an active part in the earlier petitions of 1730 in favor of the establishment of the town that would be Harvard. He must have followed with interest these early petitions, first because he had close relatives living on the land in question, and second because of a professional's concern for the matters in which he was expert—the mapping and erecting of new towns. Thus, we may surmise that Jonas Houghton noted the lack of success of these first petitions, and offered his services in support of his relatives and friends. In the latter part of 1730 his name appears at the head of the new list of petitioners, and the earliest survey of the land that would become Harvard bears his name as well.

4
MINISTERING
TO PRACTICAL MATTERS

Harvard was incorporated at a time when the New England colonies were enjoying the twentieth year of a three-decade peace—the period from the end of Queen Anne's War in 1713 to the beginning of King George's War in 1745. This peaceful interlude was accompanied by a population explosion and by rampant inflation, and both these phenomena had their effect on the farmers of the Nashua River Valley.

Most of the inhabitants of Harvard were farmers, for the economy of the town was basically agricultural, with the produce intended mostly for local consumption. There were at the time of incorporation about sixty families, representing a population of about 350, and of this number no more than five or six could call themselves millers or smiths—Peter Atherton had a blacksmith shop near his home in Still River, John Daby had a saw mill on Bowers Brook just north of Pin Hill, and a few other men had saw mills or grist mills. But most of the sixty heads of families were simply tillers of the soil. The only "industry" in town was the slate quarry on top of Pin Hill, where gravestones and other objects of stone were fabricated and in some cases exported to other communities.

The town could boast of only two public buildings—the meetinghouse, which doubled as place of worship and town hall; and the inn, which catered to gatherings of a more informal nature. There was no school or post office. There were no stores; merchandise from Boston and other trading centers was brought into town by any person who happened to be making a trip between city and country. Transportation was equally haphazard, for stagecoach lines had not yet been established.

Harvard in the mid-1730s was a small and uncomplicated community. The town, as it settled down to routine business at the beginning of 1734, took action on a number of trivial matters, projects that had to be undertaken before the town could function smoothly. A burying ground was needed, so a committee was appointed and part of the common lands granted in the previous year by the Lancaster proprietors was set off for this purpose; this cemetery, located at the center of town, served Harvard's needs for over 150 years. A pound was built for stray animals, and a set of stocks was erected for humans who might go astray. Committees were appointed periodically to "perambulate the bounds" between Harvard and each of the adjoining towns. But three matters dominated the agenda at the town meetings—the church, the school, and the highways; and the town responded in different ways to each.

The inhabitants of Harvard had spent eighteen months in erecting a meetinghouse and ordaining a minister, but their concern with the ordering of church affairs did not end there. Miscellaneous accounts for services performed and materials supplied continued to dribble in, and finally on July 14, 1737 the town asked that all accounts be brought in so that the financial oversight committee could be terminated after serving more than four years. But the settlement of old accounts was a minor problem next to the question of "seating the meetinghouse." Once the final embellishment—pews—had been installed in the meetinghouse, the question arose as to which people would sit in which pews. For three years the townspeople discussed this issue, haggling over details of social precedence, until finally a seating arrangement was determined. During these years of the mid- and late-1730s, the seating of the meetinghouse received more sustained and detailed consideration than any other item on the town's agenda.

This contrasts markedly with the treatment given the school. Repeatedly the selectmen placed on the town meeting warrant an item about the schools; some years the town chose to "leave the school with the selectmen," and some years the town took vigorous action only to reverse its decisions at a later meeting. As early as October 2, 1734, "The Town Voted to Divide the School into four Quarters," but the selectmen did not carry out this directive until January 10, 1738. Then, a year later, the town decided to keep the school at the center of the town rather than in the quarters. The town more than once voted that schoolhouses be erected in the quarters, but refused to appropriate money for that purpose. In these early years no schoolhouse was built, and apparently school was held in the meetinghouse at the center of town in some years, or at private residences in the quarters in other years. Finally in 1740, higher authorities became annoyed at Harvard's failure to comply with

An early grist mill.

Massachusetts law concerning schools; the town was called before the county court at Worcester to explain why no school had been provided for Harvard's children. Thomas Wheeler and Captain Jonathan Whitney represented the town in this matter, but the court's instructions did not have much effect, for no immediate action was taken to improve Harvard's educational facilities.

The selectmen's report of 1738 dividing the town into school quarters indicated that the population of Harvard had grown rapidly since the date of incorporation. The four quarters were "Bear" Hill, 23 families; Still River, 25 families; Old Mill, 20 families; and Oak Hill, 21 families. This total of 89 families, or about 525 persons, means that the town's population had increased by about 50 percent in a little more than five years.

The third major area of town concern was the highways. At the annual town meetings the surveyors of highways presented reports on roads to be laid out or discontinued in various parts of Harvard, and the town then proceeded to vote appropriations for maintaining the highways. The taxpayer satisfied his share of the highway rate by working a few days a year on the roads; if he were found delinquent, he would have to pay a fine in lieu of his own labor.

Highway reports consume as much space in town records as school or church matters, but in most cases the affairs of the highways were not so controversial; in only one or two cases were serious objections raised against the laying out of specific highways, and these were quickly settled by accommodating the dissatisfied parties.

School, church, and highway—these account for probably two-thirds of the material recorded in the earliest pages of the town books. Much of the remaining one-third dealt with the routine business described earlier—cemetery, pound, and similar items. These records are all evidence of an active, but somewhat narrow, concern for the affairs of the community. Only two categories of entries indicated any interest in the world beyond Harvard's boundaries: petitions for the formation of new counties; and the annual question of whether or not to send a representative to the Massachusetts House of Representatives.

Upon its incorporation Harvard was included in the county of Worcester; this county had been formed in 1731 from the western parts of Middlesex and Suffolk Counties. In 1734, 1735, and 1736 the town considered a variety of petitions to the governor and legislature in Boston, requesting that a new county be formed in the area north and west of Harvard, including Harvard and number of other Middlesex and Worcester County towns. Harvard chose to join all these petitioning groups, but none of the petitions was successful, and this wave of "new county fever" subsided.

Every May a town meeting was held to consider whether someone should be sent to speak for Harvard in the House of Representatives. The townsmen of Harvard apparently did not feel a need to be represented in the colony's legislature, for in only one of the fifteen years between the town's incorporation and 1747 was a representative chosen. In 1740 Deacon Joseph Fairbank was elected to this office, but he refused; the town's second choice was Peter Atherton, who accepted the position.

The controversy and disputation over the seating of the meetinghouse had barely died down when church and town were rocked by a scandal involving their minister, the Reverend Mr. John Seccomb. The documents relating to this incident do not record the nature of the offense, but something serious must have happened in the latter part of 1738, for on December 20 of that year a warrant was issued for a town meeting to consider a petition relating to Mr. Seccomb. The town met on the first of January, 1739, and voted that "Mr. Seccomb hath offered Christian satisfaction for his Offenses and they are reconciled to him and receive him into their Charity."

Apparently, not all the town's inhabitants were satisfied by this solution, for on February 27 the church's four deacons sent a letter to the Reverend Nathan Stone of Southborough asking for his assistance in the matter, and on March 6 another meeting was held to consider the problem. Ten men had voiced their unhappiness and their belief that Mr. Seccomb had not given sufficient satisfaction; the town upheld its previous vote, however, and no more is heard about the controversy. But the records of church proceedings, kept by Mr. Seccomb, do contain

The large mansion of Harvard's first minister, the Reverend John Seccomb, was built in 1733 near the center of town. It stood roughly on the site of the old Bromfield School and was approached through two long avenues of elm trees, one leading from the burial ground, the other from the road. Tradition also has it that Seccomb's father-in-law, Reverend William Williams of Weston, Mass., offered to furnish as large a house as Seccomb would build. The estate, consisting of the mansion and one hundred twenty acres of land, was purchased by the wealthy Boston businessman Henry Bromfield in 1765. The house burned down on August 3, 1855, though most of its contents were saved.

two short paragraphs written during the controversy and later crossed out heavily with ink. Enough can be read of one of these passages to show that it relates to the scandal, so we may conjecture that Mr. Seccomb kept a record of the progress of the dispute but attempted to remove it from the books and from people's memories after the affair was settled.

Barely six months after this curious episode, Mr. Seccomb's fortunes had reversed completely. Four young men whose religious attitudes had been a matter of concern began in September to experience a profound conversion, and in December 1739 were admitted to the church. This was the beginning of a religious revival in Harvard that would bring about one hundred new members into the fold in the following few years.

Stirrings of a religious revival had been felt in the Connecticut River Valley earlier in the decade, influenced greatly by the Reverend Jonathan Edwards, but this movement had little effect on the towns to the east. The high point of the Great Awakening, as this period of revivalism was known, did not come until 1741, with the powerful sermons of such itinerant preachers as George Whitefield and Gilbert Tennant. But Mr. Seccomb's revival preceded this high point by a full year, and this gives some indication of the sort of minister he must have been. Unlike many other ministers of the time, he was probably not content with reading his sermons from a written text that did not stir the souls and hearts of his congregation; rather, he must have had something of the evangelist in him, speaking extemporaneously and reminding his flock of the dangers of remaining unconverted.

One man whose unusual career shows the effects of this revival was Mr. John Martyn, a man who had been prominent in the affairs of Harvard since its organization. Although he had received his B.A. from Harvard College in 1724 and thus possessed many of the requirements for becoming a minister, not until 1741 did Martyn show much interest in church affairs. His spirit revived, he determined to become a minister of God, and received his M.A. from Harvard in 1743. After scouting around for a church in need of a minister, he was called by the new First Church of Northborough, and he held his post there until his death more than twenty years later.

Historians have discussed a wide variety of factors which might have caused this religious movement in the 1730s or 1740s. Among these is a theory that the young men of New England were ready for a spiritual revolution because of their difficulty in attaining economic security in a time of inflation and rapid population growth. The population of Harvard was certainly increasing precipitately during this period, and the influences of monetary inflation are seen in the yearly provision, beginning in 1740, for increases in Mr. Seccomb's salary "on

Consideration of moneys being sunk in value since [his] settlement among us."

The economic problems of the time were reflected also in the difficulties experienced in electing constables in the early 1740s. The two town constables had a variety of official duties, such as circulating the town meeting warrants, but the most important task was the collection of the various taxes—the minister's, the town's, and the county's. The town's assessors made a determination of how much each taxpayer owed, and the constable had the responsibility of collecting these amounts.

The problem for the constable was that he was responsible for delivering the full tax rate to the town treasurer whether he could collect that amount or not; any shortages had to be made up out of his own pocket. This feature of the job made it difficult enough in good times, but in times of inflation and shortages of hard currency, the constables must have been hard pressed indeed. Under these circumstances, it is not surprising that in 1741 two town meetings were required to elect nine constables, two of whom finally accepted the job.

Those men who were elected but who did not wish to be constable had two paths open to them: they could pay a fine of five pounds into the town treasury, or they could hire a replacement. In 1741 and for a year or two afterwards, the first alternative was used frequently, but by the mid-1740s the method of hiring a replacement was the only one used.

By the mid-1740s the town's religious revival had cooled down, and the difficulty in electing constables had been smoothed over; but new problems arose to demand the attention of the townspeople of Harvard. King George's War broke out in 1745, the third in a series of conflicts between the French and the English. This particular episode of the struggle was relatively short (1745–1748) and relatively tame, and was really only a prelude to the climactic French and Indian War of the following decade.

The fighting in King George's War did not threaten the Nashua River Valley; the principal theaters of war were Nova Scotia and the Champlain Valley in New York. In 1745, at least two Harvard men—William Hutchins and John Warner—were present as officers at the siege of Louisburg on Cape Breton Island, Nova Scotia; three years later a scouting party was sent out from Harvard under the command of Captain Samuel Willard, probably as a response to rumors of raiding Indians. There is no evidence that this militia band, forty of whose members were from Harvard, ever engaged in combat, and all its members returned safely.

In the midst of this conflict several residents of Shabikin, the northwest corner of Harvard, joined with some inhabitants of northern Lancaster, southwest Groton, and the remaining part of Stow Leg to try to form a new town. The petition of about 40 residents of this region surfaced in 1747, and was brought before the March 1748 town meeting. The voters of Harvard chose to reject this petition, as did the voters of the other towns concerned, and the scheme fell through. This abortive attempt to found a new town did eventually lead to the incorporation of Shirley in 1754; but only part of Groton and the remaining fragment of Stow Leg were included, Harvard and Lancaster not losing any territory. Attempts continued over the next two decades to annex parts of Harvard and Lancaster to Shirley, but without success.

Nevertheless, Shabikin for some years after was to a certain extent independent of the rest of Harvard. Its residents remained technically but not financially under the supervision of the Harvard selectmen, and apparently their children were schooled apart from other Harvard children. By 1760 the town had five highway supervisors—one for each of four districts that bore the same names as the four school quarters, and one for Shabikin. In an order of 1763 each of these surveyors was directed to provide men to clear brush from the town Common. The four larger and older districts were to provide four men each, but Shabikin was to send only two. Shabikin, a section of Harvard smaller than any of the four "quarters," had its own school district and highway supervisor; its residents apparently were not so fully integrated into the community of Harvard as were the other residents.

In 1751, four years after the Shabikin petition, a minor religious revolt began in the northeast corner of town; in June and December of that year the church held meetings to discuss what action to take in the case of a small group of persons who had broken off communion with the church. The dissidents were Samuel Mead, Ephraim Robbins, Isaac Willard, and their wives; and the actions of this small band were the first hint of much that would follow in this corner of town. One would like to know what led these few people to separate from the church, for that decision was the first in a chain of events that have given the northeastern part of Harvard a special flavor and mystique for over two hundred years, but the records are silent on their motivations.

A few years later—perhaps as early as 1754 or as late as 1760—the separatists were joined by Shadrach Ireland, a strange mystic from Charlestown. Tradition relates that Ireland had been converted by the preachings of George Whitefield, and had then gone on to develop a distinctive personal religion stressing his own immortality and the irrelevance of the marriage bond. Tradition goes on to say that his preachings in Charlestown had put him in danger of arrest by the local authorities; he chose to leave town, abandoning his wife and children, but taking with him a female companion. He settled in Harvard, finding there a number of kindred spirits. Mead, Robbins, and Willard came under his influence and others were attracted to the fold; the Square House, later taken over by the Shakers, was built by night, to be used as a place of refuge for Shadrach Ireland and as a place of assembly for all his disciples. (Ireland's stealth was occasioned by his overwhelming fear—probably unjustified—of being sought out and jailed by provincial authorities. The Square House as originally built had a cupola from which he could scan the countryside for approaching sheriffs, and secret passageways that would allow him to hide or escape at perilous moments.)

The departure of several families from Mr. Seccomb's congregation may mean that the minister's preaching had lost some of the potency of a decade earlier. Whether this be the explanation or not, the Reverend Seccomb asked for and received his dismissal from pastoral duties in Harvard. Perhaps

Shadrach Ireland's Square House. (Drawing by Bayard Underwood)

the problem lay in disagreements over the extent of the minister's "cost of living" increases in his annual salary; perhaps the rumors of a scandal involving the young maid of one of the town's prominent families had some foundation. Whatever the reason, the town found itself in the fall of 1757 looking for a new minister.

A committee of church elders undertook to manage the church in the absence of a pastor; they hired Mr. Deliverance Smith to supply the pulpit for a few Sabbaths, and on December 18, 1758, gave him a call to the ministry. Mr. Smith refused, and the committee went back to work. The second man to be called by the town and church was Mr. Joseph Wheeler; a committee conveyed their message to Mr. Wheeler on September 24, 1759, and on November 5 he accepted the call. The Reverend Wheeler was ordained on December 10, 1759, and the ad hoc steering committee of the church was dissolved.

Two years had passed since Mr. Seccomb's dismissal, but he was still a resident of Harvard, and was not to leave his elegant estate just south of the town Common for another two years. That the minister lingered on for four years after his separation from the church indicates that any scandal involving Mr.

Seccomb was not so great that he was hounded out of town. Financial considerations on Mr. Seccomb's part were also not a likely explanation for his dismissal; a four-year vacation without pay hints at considerable financial security.

There were many people in town, however, who were not so well off financially. From time to time a person or family in town might suffer an economic setback, or become physically incapable of self-support, and in these cases the town could be very generous. In 1749 the town granted one acre of the common land just east of the meetinghouse to John Wright and his wife, and made arrangements to erect a house on this lot. But John Wright died in 1752, and his wife in 1754, leaving behind an acre of land with a houseframe on it. After some haggling this structure was bought by the town and turned over to Joseph Blood for the use of his family. Joseph Blood had been receiving town relief since 1746, and from time to time the town voted him and his family a cow or some other necessary article. That these were the only two "welfare cases" on the town records for a thirty-year period is evidence that Harvard's farmers were for the most part successful and self-sufficient.

On occasion individuals or families moving into Harvard would threaten to become a burden to the town. With these people the town was not so generous, and had an instrument for dealing with them—the institution of "warning out." Under Massachusetts law, a town had to provide relief to any person demanding it, provided that person had resided in town for six months without being asked to leave. If the selectmen learned of a recent arrival who might be in need of support, they would send the constable to warn this person out of town. In most cases those so warned did not leave town, but the formal action of the selectmen protected the town's treasury from drainage in this direction. The town records contain dozens of notices of warning out, starting almost from the day of Harvard's incorporation; the town fathers were diligent indeed in managing the community funds entrusted to them.

In 1754 began the French and Indian War, the final phase in the struggle between French and English for control of the North

American continent. Expeditions were sent annually to Nova Scotia and the Champlain Valley, and Harvard men took part in these campaigns every summer from 1754 to 1760. The fighting was mostly over by the latter year, but the peace did not come until 1763; in the intervening three years, Harvard residents served on garrison duty at Louisburg, Ticonderoga, and other critical points. The fighting did not come near Harvard territory, but the war had a number of lasting effects on the town.

Two militia companies had been formed in town in response to the repeated demand for manpower during the war. Peter Atherton was captain of the first company, and Phinehas Fairbank was captain of the second. These two companies were not disbanded in 1763, but enjoyed a continuous existence through the Revolution and well into the nineteenth century.

Continued concern about the events of the war had turned the attention of the townspeople to the outside world more than at any previous time. This change in perspective may have been one of the factors leading the inhabitants of Harvard to choose more often to send a delegate to the House of Representatives. Having sent only one representative in the years prior to 1747, the town chose a representative in six of the years from 1747 through 1763. From 1764 onward, Harvard was represented at the General Court in most years.

The conclusion of hostilities with the French opened for settlement vast areas to the north and west. One of the new towns to arise in the 1760s was the old grant of Dorchester Canada, a tract of land given to the heirs of soldiers in the first French conflict of the 1690s. Many of the heirs and descendants of these earlier French and Indian fighters had settled in Lancaster and Harvard, and in the 1760s some of these families migrated to Dorchester Canada, which soon became the town of Ashburnham. In this way Harvard lost about twenty families, led by Thomas Wheeler, one of the principal petitioners for incorporation in 1730.

Even with this significant loss of families, the town's population continued to increase; the provincial census of 1765 credited Harvard with 1,126 inhabitants, more than a three-fold increase in thirty years. This number would increase somewhat over the following few decades, but the town would not experience another period of such population increase until 200 years later.

In many ways the town was unchanged from the 1730s. Most of the inhabitants were farmers, producing enough to live comfortably, but not much more. The school system had become stabilized, being kept sometimes in the center of town and sometimes in the quarters; as yet no schoolhouse had been erected. A curious group of schismatics, not really a church, were still operating in the northeast corner of town; but most of the townspeople were members of the one fully organized church, the Congregational.

But change was in the air. An increased population meant more highways and more communication with the outside world. This general increase in awareness of external affairs would, in the ensuing years, revamp the ways of the town. The economy would become more diversified, and the people would have a choice among several places of worship. More and more often town meetings would consider problems that went beyond the town's boundaries.

One small set of circumstances will serve to illustrate the impending events that would restructure the town. In 1765, Henry Bromfield, a wealthy merchant from Boston, bought Mr. John Seccomb's mansion and for several years used the estate as a summer residence. Within a few years, the young Reverend William Emerson, minister of the church at Concord, began to make occasional trips to Harvard, visiting the Reverend Mr. Wheeler or Mr. Bromfield; these trips were the first of many associations between the Emerson family and the town of Harvard. These two men—Mr. Bromfield the merchant, and Mr. Emerson the minister—represented a world of ideas, both sacred and secular, previously unknown to Harvard—ideas that would have a lasting impact on the town.

§ A Sabbath Journal

In 1942 Walt Harris, a resident of Woodchuck Hill Road in Harvard and a member of the Harvard Historical Society, wrote the following fictional journal entry, ascribing it to John Martyn, prominent citizen of Harvard in the 1730s. "This is all I was able to copy upon that first visit," Harris concludes his effort, "and all apparently that will ever be known of John Martyn's Journal"—but by his own confession he had actually made up the entire entry. Harris, a commercial artist with a consuming interest in the details of life in early Harvard, probably based his journal style on the famous diary of Judge Samuel Sewall of Salem; though it is not historically impeccable, it does offer a lively picture of a Harvard Sabbath in 1736.

JOHN MARTYN
His Journal.

(Entry.) May, the first day, in the Year 1736. AnnoDom.
The Lord's Day.

I, John Martyn, being 30 years old this last May 10th, blessed by Divine Providence with good health and young strength, and some measure of the goods of this world, having but lately come to Harvard, the new Town, from Boston, herein do purpose to sett down the things which surround my daily life in a place much removed from the sea. This journal being recommended to me by my father's good friend Justice Sewall, who keeps such a record.

Since Mary, my wife, suffers from an affliction of the breathing much aggrivated by easte winds, and in part since we are both desirous of greater quiet than is possible in a seaport town where at times Bands of drunken sailors ashore make the nights riotous. Then, too, do we escape from overmuch talk of witchcraft which infamy still persists: Mainly, then, for an idyllic life.

Moreover, this town endears itself to me by reason of various who were college friends at Cambridge and indeed these associations are so strong as to have named this town "Harvard." Thus are we favored by friendly visitors during those seasons when the ways are not impassable.

The house in which we live is ancient even in this new Town and much browned by the seasons, having been solidly built many years ago. The fields and garden grounds about it are well watered by springs and brooks, well sunned and productive. Thus with the help of my negro servant, Cato, we can garner and store ample produce against lean times and deep winter. . . .

Thus, then, this cheerful June Sabbath morning do we note the sun mark on the kitchen floor and sett out for Meeting, Cato have the horse saddled and pillioned for our journey and tied by the mounting stone. Cato to stay and attend the house, the baby and fire along with such pots as may be cooking. I mounted the horse and holding the basket of midday victuals helped Mary to get up behind me.

We go along the highway but newly cleared by the town to the Meeting House and all along the common ground, after which the road goes to Groton. The warming sun cast its long beams between the tall trees, some of them giant pitch pines marked by the broad arrow of His Majestie the King, and brought sweet scents from the earth and growing things. Amidst the bosks and bush a chorus of birds. We had but lost the house to view when two Indians appeared across the path carrying a slain deer upon a shoulder pole. The arrow was still showing its feathering just in front of the left fore shoulder. They nodded in silence and passed on their way to their camp near Mr. Willard's meadow where is their familiar place at this season.

The waters are not yet all gone down and we are putt to holding our Sunday shoes above the flood at the ford. Many fish could be seen to dart away to shadowy hiding. Numbers of quail and now and then a turkey flew up in noise, and long legged cranes straightened their crooked necks at our passing.

The day being clear distant blue hills could be seen from high ground and through the trees, this being most pleasing and somehow in accord with our Sabbath journey. Because of much hills and great numbers of trees in this country side, the scattered houses are not seen from afar and so we are in suddenness arrived at the Grand Parsonage and to the Burial Ground and the broad Common Plain and thence but shortly over the rise and to the Meeting House below having gathered with us by now various others on the way.

The Meeting House, of which we are proud in possession, still has the look of new cut wood with those stains which are rust from nails in the claveboards or clapboards. It sits pleasantly in the sunshine and looks across a little valley wherein is the narrow part of Stow boundary being called the Leg and along which is a Highway to the Meeting House.

There will be for our meeting more bodily comfort than many of those of the cold winter for now is no need of foot warmer filled with hot coals from a neighboring hearth.

The wide door stands open, it is still early; the drummer has but just sounded the first roll, and yet most are here for to be early gives time to learn those things of the locality which are fitting to know and some perchance which must need be spoken in whispers and as asides. The heavy leg stocks newly fashioned by Mr. Daby, and empty of culprit, as always here, are thus placed by Colonial Law. Also must this place house all meetings both of God and Mammon, with, in season, school for the young that they may acquire knowledge to conduct themselves as God Fearing citizens in Life. A school house being planned for next year. In that the law forbids all unneedful labor on the Sabbath, both Church and State, and indicates the duty of church and tythes are present but those infirm or sick.

I saw one by name of Mercy Daby who by reason of running afoul a noxious vine, plentiful all about, was swollen of face and hands and whose visible person shone with the soft soap with which she had annointed herself in order to stay the discomfort of the poison. But most were rugged and strong and bronze of face, and all befitting the day. . . .

But to the Meeting House for now is the last drum roll, and as all enter, men to one side, women to the other, I glance at Mary as we part and observe her examine discreetly the new fine clothing of Mistress Seccomb, just to her fore in entering, that lady being beautiful but cold. The unaccustomed Sunday shoes squeak across the wide board floor and there is some clearing of throats. Deacons Stone and Daby, well presenting that attitude which gives forth the term "pillars of the church," stiffly each takes his place. I am by the pulpit stairs. The grading of Dignity as to Seats is a matter of no small importance, since herein, also, must be considered how great contribution is made toward this Meeting House. The subject calls out many and intimate personal things and discussions with heat of temper. Four pews at front will face the body of the church and each carefully accorded its occupants. In this I am done much honor. Twelve pews to fill the lower floor and these look toward the altar. These, too, are graded as to rightful sitting.

The light of day comes greenishly through the square panes of glass and casts its beams over the sober people. Jonathan Crouch, the tythingman, in scarf of office, takes his observant post with wand close to hand that he may foster quiet and attention in judicial solemnity. I envy him not his none too pleasing task of tax and tythe gathering; it savors but little of generous friendliness. Yet here is one who broadly must be severe toward individuals in that community to succeed, and stern and large of frame he sees but duty to be done.

The minister now turns the sand glass upon his desk and gravely begins the familiar service of the church. The congregation answers in its part. A hymn quite well known to all is read aloud by the singing leader—book and tuning fork in hand. Given the pitch of tone the people sing slowly and sonorously while standing. Seated once more with some rattle of wooden seats, the congregation settles back for the long prayer and beginning of the day's sermon.

Mr. Seccomb had chosen Ecclesiastes 7:15. "For the hope of the Un-Godly is like Dust that is Blown Away by the Wind," and made a masterly sermon the effect of which still surges within me. The man is a master of powerful argument and individual in ideas.

It was during midday respite and the partaking in company of our prepared victuals, that such news and reports as had not been before passed out or about, then gave interest, yet but little of levity among all. There did appear anxiety among some as to the safety of horses from thieves since a nearby place had been thus affected. And these would have each horse marked by heated iron with a device of true ownership either as of town or individual.

It was after such partaking of food that Meeting resumed and Master Crouch's task became less lightsome, since various, unused to indoor air and overly fed must needs be aroused to a wakeful piety by admonishing taps upon shoulder and head. Nor did his well greased shoes give warning nor disturb the minister's tenthly passages; these by now having reached that point where said ungodly began to sense, even smell, the burning pit!

Thus with the tonic of old familiar hymns sung forth, psalm, prayer and benediction comes to a close another Sabbath service. Handshakings and we start for our homes. The sun has begun to cast long shafts of light and like shadows, nor do we tarry long since many tasks await before deep darkness and the bed. For in this removed place our living calls for dawn to dark labor and he is laggard who clings to his morning pillow while about, all are laboring that each may fill his part for that good of all.

We part, one after another, with those of our way, and at length do we come to our familiar old house, its windows agleam from the sun. Cato comes a running to take the horse and Mary at once to the baby. Between us we do all those things against the morrow and Mary and I to eat our simple pudding. Then before the broad hearth, its fire low and yet enough of daylight that I may write. And indeed my interest is such that I find darkness fallen and need of candle so that I must end and ashe the fire. And now am I sure that at this rate of writing, I cannot hope to attain but seldom, but rather to sett down in much more brief the happenings of my days, Nor do I forget this Sabbath Day the Blessings of God. Amen—and so to bed.

§ John Seccomb, Minister

The Reverend John Seccomb's career in Harvard gives evidence that he was not typical of New England ministers in the early decades of the eighteenth century. He seems to have lived a life of contradictions—at times he was in deep trouble because of rumors of a scandal of undefined nature; at other times he was the leader of a religious revival which attracted many unregenerates to the church. What is known of his life in the years before and after his residence at Harvard? Was John Seccomb, as seen by the townfolk of Harvard from 1732 to 1761, the same John Seccomb seen in other communities?

Seccomb was born in Malden on April 25, 1708, the son of Peter Seccomb and Hannah Willis. He entered Harvard College with the class of 1728 and had a most interesting undergraduate career. He was in frequent trouble for participation in a variety of pranks, such as conspiring with four other undergraduates to kidnap a goose from Cambridge Common. Despite these disciplinary problems he graduated with his class and remained at the college, taking advantage of a number of postgraduate scholarships. His appetite for the more frivolous side of college life does not seem to have diminished in these postgraduate years. In a letter of 1729 to a schoolmate who had already obtained a ministerial post, Seccomb maintained a jocular and decidedly nonpuritanical tone throughout as he transmitted the latest gossip about who was caught playing cards or who was seen in the company of certain young widows of Cambridge. Seccomb was also a master of nonsense verse, the most famous example being a piece called "Father Abbey's Will," a parody of the pretentious will of Matthew Abdy, the poor college sweeper. This bit of poetry has been reprinted many times, and has even been set to music.

John Seccomb's leisurely life at Cambridge was interrupted early in 1733 by the invitation to come to Harvard as the town's minister. Chapter Four discusses his three decades in Harvard, culminating in his dismissal from his ministerial post in 1757. He was very soon invited to join a group of New Englanders who were about to leave for Nova Scotia to settle a new town in that recently conquered province. He preached his first sermon at Chester, Nova Scotia on August 9, 1759, and returned to settle permanently after selling his Harvard mansion in 1761. In the remaining years before the Revolution he divided his time between Chester and Halifax, ministering to more than one congregation, but without a settled salary.

At the outbreak of the Revolution, the Reverend Seccomb preached a sermon in support of the rebellious colonies which brought him into conflict with the loyalist forces in Nova Scotia. He was not, however, removed from the pulpit, but continued to preach until his death in 1792.

John Seccomb lived only three of his eight decades in Harvard. His long and eventful life shows that from beginning to end he was a vital force among his colleagues and neighbors. Whether at Harvard College, or in the town of Harvard, or in Chester, Nova Scotia, he was constantly in conflict with the authorities, while at the same time earning the love and respect of classmates and parishioners. Above all, he retained an open mind and a lively sense of humor. His biography in Sibley's *Harvard Graduates* states that even in old age he "had never lost the humor of the lad who wrote nonsense verse."

5
BEYOND TOWN BORDERS

At first glance the issues confronting the inhabitants of Harvard in the late 1760s did not differ greatly from the issues of the preceding two or three decades. Town meeting warrants continued to carry the same items on appropriations for schools and highways, and on the perennial question of whether or not the swine should run at large (always answered in the affirmative). A closer look, though, shows that although the issues were much the same, the method of dealing with some of these issues had altered significantly. A striking example would be the handling of highway disputes; as long as highways had been laid out, there had always been someone who felt that he had been injured by the choice of location. In the first few decades of Harvard's existence, these disputes had been handled internally, by submitting the problem to arbitration by the selectmen or an ad hoc committee of disinterested townsmen. But by the end of the 1760s this had changed; disgruntled Harvard residents with highway grievances took their complaints to the county court in Worcester, and several such cases are seen in the minutes of the town meetings. This use of the county courts for the solution of internal problems is symptomatic of the partial disintegration of a closeknit and partially isolated New England community, but may also be viewed as an emerging willingness on the part of individual townspeople to look beyond the limited horizons of the town's boundaries.

A different facet of this same tendency is seen in the increasing attention paid to provincial and continental affairs. The first incident that appears to have drawn the attention of the people of Harvard was the turmoil surrounding the attempt to implement the Stamp Act. On December 1, 1766 the town instructed its representative to the General Court to use his influence to obtain reparations for those in Boston who had suffered during the Stamp Act disturbances; the exact amount of these reparations was left to the discretion of the representative, in consultation with his colleagues.

Pre-Revolutionary rumblings continued in 1767 when the town concurred with a vote of the town of Boston limiting imports and encouraging domestic manufacture. A year later, Israel Taylor was sent as the town's delegate to a convention at Boston, and the town adopted a resolution declaiming its constitutional rights. The town records do not show any further dealings with the affairs of empire until 1772, but the town did send a representative to Boston regularly through this period, with the single exception of the year 1770.

In the midst of these concerns with external affairs, the townsmen of Harvard were confronted for the second time with a vacancy in the pulpit. In May of 1767 Mr. Wheeler announced his temporary "absence," but it soon became apparent that he was seriously ill and would not be able to fulfill his ministerial duties. Negotiations leading to Mr. Wheeler's dismissal consumed more than a year, seemingly without rancor on either side. Finally, on July 28, 1768, Mr. Wheeler was formally dismissed from his position and the search for a replacement began.

Even before Mr. Wheeler's dismissal, a suggestion had been made to obtain the services of the Reverend John Emerson, preacher at Malden (brother of the Reverend William Emerson, preacher at Concord and friend to Col. Henry Bromfield of Harvard), but there is no evidence that an actual offer was ever made. In December 1768 the town and the church issued a call to Mr. Daniel Johnson to settle with them as minister, but the following month he declined the offer. In June 1769 the call to Mr. Johnson was renewed, and this time he accepted. He was ordained on November 1, 1769.

In 1770, not many months after the ordination of Mr. Johnson, the question was put at town meeting whether a new meetinghouse should be built. Harvard's population had increased dramatically since 1732, and the old meetinghouse could no longer accommodate all those who wished to attend religious services or town meetings. The answer in 1770 was no, but two years later the issue appeared again, and this time the decision was made to proceed with the construction of a larger meetinghouse. The changing mode of conducting town business is as evident in the building of this meetinghouse as it had been evident for some years in the resolution of highway disputes. The erection of the first meetinghouse in 1733 had been a community project in the widest sense. Every decision was made directly by the town meeting or a committee appointed by the meeting; every able-bodied inhabitant was expected to contribute a fair share of his labor; probably half or more of the townsmen submitted bills for materials supplied or services performed during the construction period. But now, in 1772, the sense of community was not so strong; discussions about the plans for the building continued through the winter of 1772–73, until in a meeting of April 5, 1773, the town voted to build "by the great"—in other words, to let out contracts. The first person to be granted a contract was Oliver Atherton, who agreed to terms whereby he would construct the frame of the building, once the underpinning had been laid.

Before ground could be broken, however, the people interested in the project had to agree on the location of the new structure. At first the town voted to place the new meetinghouse just south of the old; then they voted to reconsider this vote. On May 31, 1773 the town met on a warrant which included an article dealing with the location of the meetinghouse. Apparently the arguments had boiled down to a dispute over two sites, for the meeting was adjourned temporarily and those in attendance were instructed to proceed to one or the other of two spots and place a stone there, thus indicating their preferences. When everyone had voted, the two piles were counted, and were found to contain the same number of "ballots." The town meeting minutes do not tell how this impasse was overcome, but the final decision was to place the new meetinghouse just south of the old one, as had been voted some months before.

Construction proceeded smoothly during the summer of 1773; the project was a curious mixture of newfangled, businesslike contracts and old-fashioned communal contributions. In June 1773, while Oliver Atherton and his crew were busy knocking together the frame of the building, the town was attempting to arrange provisioning for the 160 men who would be needed to raise the frame once it was built. This festive occasion must have occurred before July 17, for on that date the town accepted Atherton's frame, and considered accounts for expenses at the raising of the meetinghouse. The community had come together briefly for the raising, but then more contracts were let for doing the finish-work; the town passed on each of these contracts, requiring some of the contractors to make up deficiencies in their work. By the end of 1773 all that was left was a bit of landscaping around the completed building; this last effort was made in the spring of 1774, and by May of that year the project was at an end.

The decision to erect a new meetinghouse brought with it two additional problems for the townspeople to consider—how to allocate the new pews, and what to do with the old meetinghouse. More time was spent at town meetings deciding how to sell the pews than was spent on planning the construction of the meetinghouse. Once the house was built and the pews sold, it was necessary to confront the problem of who would sit in which pews. As usual, a committee was chosen for that purpose, and on January 2, 1775 the committee report on seating the meetinghouse was read at town meeting and accepted by the voters.

The problem of the old meetinghouse was not so routine as that of arranging seating. The first decision was simply to tear down the old building, but this was quickly reconsidered. A committee was appointed in October 1774 to arrange for the sale of the old meetinghouse; on March 6, 1776 the committee reported that the old building had been sold for fourteen pounds, nineteen shillings, and fourpence. Between these two dates the leader of the town's "minute band" proposed that the pews be removed from the obsolete structure and that the empty shell be used for militia training during inclement weather, but this suggestion was not adopted.

The old meetinghouse was sold to a group from the eastern side of Harvard and the adjoining parts of Littleton and Stow who wanted to set up their own church; in 1776, barely a year after their purchase of a place of worship (which they moved to the eastern part of Harvard), this group petitioned the General Court to be erected as a new township. The town of Harvard was, not surprisingly, opposed to this idea, and its reply to the petition provides ample evidence of the unsettled state of the Harvard community.

In opposing the petition, the townsmen of Harvard expressed a fear that if a group from the eastern side of town were allowed to separate, those on the west would want the same privilege. This undoubtedly refers to those of Shabikin who more than twenty years earlier had tried to include themselves in the formation of Shirley. They had petitioned again in 1768 to be joined to Shirley, and this statement of the Harvard town meeting indicates that secessionist feelings continued in Shabikin ten years later.

The bill of particulars against the petition from those on the east side of town continues with the observation that a Baptist Society had lately been set up in town, and that as a result those who still adhered to the First Church were experiencing more and more difficulty in supporting their minister. On June 27, 1776, fourteen persons under the leadership of Dr. Isaiah Parker founded the Baptist church in Still River. Dr. Parker was a man of many talents; a physician by profession, he was Baptist minister from 1778 to 1798, when he converted to the Universalist persuasion. The Baptists at this early date were a small congregation, but to those who remained faithful to the First Church, this new religious group was another threat to the solidarity of the Harvard community.

The bill of particulars did not mention one other fractious

group within the bounds of Harvard at that time—Shadrach Ireland and his disciples. Very little is known about this group, but they were still active in the 1770s, some twenty years after their first appearance. At a town meeting of December 15, 1777, the townspeople of Harvard voted to free Isaac Willard, Zaccheus Stevens, and Abijah Worster—three of Ireland's adherents—from paying minister's rates, because they had produced a "certificate . . . that they belong to some other religious society."

The business of erecting a new meetinghouse, of reseating the meetinghouse, or of dealing with disintegrative elements within the community was not an annual feature of the town's existence; but these problems had been encountered before, and precedents existed for dealing with them. During these same years, different and more extraordinary problems arose, for which there was no prior experience; these were of course the string of incidents which led up to the American Revolution. A few of these had already been experienced in the years 1766, 1767, and 1768. As far as Harvard was concerned, there were no further occurrences of this sort until 1773; but from that year, records of town actions give evidence of increasing involvement in pre-Revolutionary activities, culminating in the open rebellion of 1775 and later years.

The town's first Committee of Correspondence was chosen in March 1773; these three men, who would communicate with similar groups in other towns in order to coordinate policy in this time of crisis, were Mr. Joseph Wheeler (the town's second minister), and two deacons—Oliver Whitney and Phinehas Fairbank. This committee immediately sent a letter to its counterpart in Boston, praising it and thanking it for its guidance. Later that year the Committee of Correspondence and the town responded to the Boston Tea Party by proposing and voting a set of resolves which supported the actions of the Bostonians, discountenanced the use of imported tea, and declaimed the rights of British subjects in the matter of taxation.

The Boston Tea Party led of course to the enactment of the Boston Port Bill of June 1, 1774, by which Parliament closed the port of Boston to all shipping. This provided another opportunity for the town to proclaim its revolutionary sentiments, and to deliver these sentiments to the leaders in Boston.

In the wake of these tumultuous events, the royally appointed authorities in Boston suspended the meetings of the House of Representatives; the independent-minded townspeople arranged for an extralegal Provincial Congress to be held at Concord in October 1774. Mr. Joseph Wheeler was chosen as Harvard's delegate to this congress, and to many later gatherings of a similar nature, both statewide and countywide.

On April 19, 1775 the nature of the conflict was changed profoundly. Many Harvard men responded to the Concord and Lexington alarms, some procuring weapons and ammunition from the common store kept at the meetinghouse. When these men returned to Harvard after their march to Cambridge and other points, the caretakers of the town's supplies of war attempted to repossess these borrowed armaments, but without much success.

Harvard men served also in various of the campaigns which constituted the siege of Boston. Service in these campaigns, as in

A minuteman responding to the call.

the earlier French and Indian Wars, was calculated in weeks and months, and was not spoken of as an enlistment. Later in the war, when attempts were made by the town to remunerate its own soldiers, various men of Harvard were awarded sums for their participation, for example, in the Roxbury campaign of 1775 (six weeks), or in the Dorchester campaign (two months).

At this early stage of the hostilities, the available records present no indication that Harvard's participants anticipated a long conflict. From April 1775 to July 1776 or even later, the actions of the townspeople were obviously based on expectations that the fighting would soon be over. Weapons were temporarily borrowed from the town's supply; participation in actual soldiering was limited to very short periods.

A change in attitudes can be observed, however, throughout the latter half of 1775, in so simple a place as the formalized heading to the town meeting warrants. For as long as people could remember, these warrants had been legitimized by invoking the king's power; warrants issued to the constables by the selectmen began "In His Majesties name, you are hereby required" and so forth. As 1775 wore on, this invocation was qualified by noting that the calling of the town meetings was based upon many years of "local custom and usage," thus diminishing to some extent the legitimizing power of the crown. By December 1775, the king's name had been dropped completely, and warrants were issued instead for "the service of the Province of Massachusetts Bay." Half a year before the Declaration of Independence the townspeople of Harvard had dispensed with this one small symbol of dependence upon royal authority.

As it became more evident that the colonists could not win their independence in a few months only, the call went out for men to enlist for three years in the Continental Army. Harvard was enjoined to provide its share of soldiers on several occasions, and was able to comply each time, although more than once recourse was taken to the common and accepted practice of hiring outsiders to fill the town's quota.

Each year the town was called upon to make increasingly large appropriations for war charges, and for the most part the money appears to have been raised without great difficulty. Many years would pass before the constables, treasurers, and taxpayers had settled all accounts and collected back taxes; but when the money was needed, it was forthcoming.

The people of Harvard had other pressing problems during these years of revolution. Most immediately, the Declaration of Independence had left all the colonies without an acknowledged framework of government. In Massachusetts, a call soon went out for the assembly of a state constitutional convention. The town of Harvard joined in this call; the town meetings of September 1776 and May 1777 instructed their representative at the Provincial Congress to press for such a convention. A draft of the constitution was circulated in 1778, at which time Harvard's voters expressed their dissatisfaction with a number of particular articles, but their willingness to accept the document as a whole. By mid-1780 the state constitution had been ratified, and in September of that year the town voted for the first time for state officers—governor, lieutenant governor, and counsellors and senators.

Closer to home, Harvard found itself for the third time without a preacher. In the excitement of the summer of 1775, the Reverend Mr. Johnson and the men of Colonel Asa Whitcomb's regiment had asked that Mr. Johnson be temporarily relieved of his post in Harvard so that he might become chaplain to the regiment during its participation in the siege of Boston. The town would not allow this, for fear of losing its young minister. But in the summer of 1776 Mr. Johnson somehow managed to have his way, and joined the troops in the field. A year later he was dead, and the townspeople of Harvard once again undertook to search out a replacement. The times being unsettled, four years would pass before the next minister was ordained at Harvard.

During these years also the residents of the eastern side of Harvard, in conjunction with people in adjoining parts of Littleton and Stow, continued their agitation for their own small piece of independence. As noted above, Harvard's voters had rejected the first petition to this end, but these petitioners were in 1778

Early cider mill.

erected into the parish of Boxborough. Harvard's opposition melted slowly, and in 1783 Boxborough moved a step closer to being a full-fledged town, attaining the status of a district.

In 1781 Harvard's quota for providing three-year enlistees for the Continental Army was sixteen; there must have been some difficulty in filling the quota in this year, for a new and different mode of raising the men was attempted. The assessors, the selectmen, and eight other trusted inhabitants were appointed to arrange the town's taxpayers into sixteen groups in such a way that each group would, taken as a whole, be of approximately equal wealth with respect to each other group. When this was done each of the sixteen "classes" was instructed to act independently to engage one man for the Continental Army. This technique appears to have worked, but it laid the foundations for years of litigation and disputation; the sixteen groups varied in their ability or willingness to make good their promised payments to the men they had encouraged to enlist, and the unpaid enlistees did not accept this state of affairs.

War appropriations of increasing magnitude and frequency continued well into 1781, but it is difficult to know just how much was spent on account of the rampant wartime inflation. As an example, the appropriation for schools in pre-Revolutionary years was usually about 75 pounds, but in 1780 was 18,000 pounds. In that same year war appropriations of 20,000 pounds, 80,000 pounds, 30,000 pounds (for beef), and 3,200 pounds were voted. As usual, these levies could be satisfied with contributions of agricultural produce; the money equivalent of rye used for soldiers' pay was set at 70 pounds per bushel.

Harvard's affairs began to return to normal in the middle of 1781, some months before Yorktown. The last war appropriation was voted in July 1781. The lengthy warrant for the March election meeting of 1782 contained no war-related items, although later meetings that year had to face difficulties arising out of the war-generated financial entanglements.

For six years Harvard had contended with the problems of war, and for some years before that with lesser problems of an unusual nature. Throughout this period the townspeople were also confronted with the ongoing routines and discomforts of small-town life in the eighteenth century. Smallpox epidemics had swept the area; there were five pock hospitals in Worcester County alone, one of them located in Lancaster very near the Still River bridge. Though inoculation with smallpox vaccine was widespread, graves in Harvard's burying grounds attest to the grim losses many families sustained.

Merchants in both Harvard and Still River continued to be licensed by the town to sell retail goods, usually from rooms in their homes that were designated for the purpose. There was a larger general store in each village; retired clergyman Squire Joseph Wheeler ran one of these, and the Haskell family, who would dominate the Still River retail scene until the middle of the nineteenth century, ran the smaller one. Some of these merchants as well as some farmers obtained licenses to serve as innkeepers throughout this period; their establishments, usually providing simple fare and accommodations in their own homes, were permitted to serve liquor and served as stopping points for thirsty stagecoach travelers or mail carriers.

Apple orchards flourished on family farms; at least twenty farmers each produced from thirty to forty barrels of cider a year, most of it for their own use. A tannery functioned in town; and in the later 1700s Harvard had three active works for the production of potash, an increasingly important commodity in the region.

The constables continued to warn out of town strangers who threatened to become a burden on the town's treasury. The town records are, on the other hand, scattered with entries indicating a concern for the welfare of those inhabitants of

Harvard who had come upon hard times, including continued support of the family of Joseph Blood. In 1777 Joseph Blood died, and the cow that had been maintained for his support was sold.

The school continued to be held regularly, its appropriations routinely voted at every March meeting. Apparently school was kept in the quarters, for in 1783, after years of silence on the subject, the town voted not to keep school in the middle of town, and not to change the present method of keeping school. At the March meeting a year later, the first school district was established in the middle of town, covering the area within a one-mile radius of the meetinghouse. The rest of the town was undistricted, and would remain so for a number of years.

Year after year the town voted to have the surveyors of highways expend a certain amount of time clearing brush from the Common and the burying yard. Twice the town commissioned surveys of the Common, once in 1775 and again in 1782. These investigations revealed that the original grant of thirty acres from the Lancaster proprietors had been reduced to sixteen and a half acres; the land had been dissipated by sale, gift, and encroachment. The report of 1782 made a careful inventory of these encroachments, and over the next few years the town came to terms with all the offenders. In some cases the landgrabbers were allowed to purchase the lands; in others they graciously returned the land to the town. The increasing concern of the townspeople for the preservation of this open space in the center of town is evident in an order of 1783, which requires those providing wood for the minister to gather the wood from the Common, but reserve some trees for shade.

Harvard had been without a minister since Mr. Johnson's death in 1777, but with the return to normality, a call went out in early 1782 to Mr. Ebenezer Grosvenor, a native of Pomfret, Connecticut, who had for some years been minister at Scituate. Mr. Grosvenor accepted and once more Harvard's pulpit had a settled occupant; the ordination took place on June 19, 1782.

In the meantime Shadrach Ireland had died, in the summer of 1780. His followers believed in his immortality and did not

A marble slab in the woods off South Shaker Road marks the spot where two elders were beaten by an angry mob. Shaker custom when passing by was to place a stone on the cairn in memory of the incident. (Courtesy Fruitlands Museums)

bury him immediately. In a few days, however, his mortality became all too obvious, and Ireland's body was taken into a cornfield in the dead of night and buried without a trace.

The remaining members of the society attempted to carry on in the old manner, but without their longtime leader they would have soon dispersed, had not Mother Ann Lee and her band of Shakers arrived in Harvard in the following year. Ann Lee and a number of her followers had left England in 1774 and taken ship for New York. They settled in the wilderness just west of Albany, but had not attracted many converts until the summer of 1780, when they were discovered by a group from New Lebanon, New York, who a year earlier had experienced one of the last flickerings of the Great Awakening. The newly swelled band of Believers decided to tour New England in 1781, and one of their first stops was Harvard.

After a brief stop at the home of Zaccheus Stevens in Still

River, Mother Ann and company moved on to the Square House in the northeast corner of town. Soon they were attracting interested observers from the neighboring towns—both potential converts and potential troublemakers. In 1781 and again in 1783 the town voted that the selectmen escort the "shaking Quakers" out of Harvard. This was not done by the selectmen, but on at least two occasions mobs took decisive action. In 1782 the Shakers were driven out of town, only to return; the following year a mob bound and whipped a number of the Believers, but still they were not discouraged. Eventually the violent opposition died down and the Shakers became a fixed feature of the town.

In 1782 Aaron Jewett, acting for the Shakers, purchased the Square House from the heirs of Shadrach Ireland; and in 1787 the "Society that attends the Public Worship at Capt. Aaron Jewett's" was freed from paying its school rates, so that it might keep a school of its own. Some of the remnant of Ireland's group were absorbed into the Shaker band, and the northeast section of town maintained its reputation as a haven for advocates of unorthodox beliefs.

For a quarter of a century the inhabitants of Harvard had been besieged by a wide range of issues crying for attention—they had made their contribution to the fighting of the Revolution and had offered suggestions for the framing of state and federal constitutions; they had built a new meetinghouse and twice had sought out and obtained new ministers; they had dealt repeatedly with the recurring details of small-town life. As this period drew to a close, the people of Harvard witnessed in 1787 the ratification of a new federal system of government, and in 1788 they voted for the first time for presidential electors and for a representative in the national government. And in May 1788, the town's fourth minister, the Reverend Ebenezer Grosvenor, died at the age of 49; once again the town had to call upon its reserves of communal energy, and begin the search for a replacement in the pulpit.

§ The Old Burial Grounds

Harvard's original burial ground was granted to the town by the Lancaster proprietors in 1733—just one year after the town's incorporation. The first burial was that of a child, Elizabeth Willard; the first stone memorial was the one placed over the grave of Ephraim Stone, who died on July 16, 1734. The earliest gravemarkers are all of the blue slate that was quarried on Pin Hill. Slate from that quarry was probably used for gravestones in other nearby towns as well, and in the eighteenth and early nineteenth centuries the quarrying and carving of slate for gravestones was one of Harvard's minor but indispensable industries.

"Some of the workmen kept in stock a collection of head and foot stones, assorted sizes, set up in a grim row by the roadside to attract purchasers," wrote Henry Nourse in his 1894 *History of Harvard*. "These ready-made memorials were finished even to the lugubrious willow drooping over 'HERE LIES,' above the blank space of the inscription; and always had some sententious legend at the base—entirely non-committal and available for any character saintly or reprobate—such as 'An honest man's the noblest work of God,' or 'Death levels all both the Wicked and the Just.' "

Nourse also reports that many of the town's earliest residents—Willards, Athertons, Houghtons, Warners, etc.—were not buried in the cemetery, but rather in the older burial grounds in the towns of Groton, Stow, and Lancaster; and that many of the earliest burials in Harvard's cemetery were unmarked by gravestones.

The consistency in style of the lettering and decoration of the slate gravestones erected from the 1730s until about the 1760s suggests that no more than one or two local craftsmen were then involved in carving stone. The very first stones had no decoration other than a simple lined border; the inscriptions were in small, neat capital letters. But by the 1740s nearly all the stones have the same characteristic shape and design. A stark, simple death's head adorned the semicircular top of the stone; the borders were decorated with scrolls and other circular figures; the inscriptions were now in script, not just block letters; and the sides of the stones, rather than descending to the ground in parallel, tapered towards one another slightly—suggesting to some the shape of the coffins used in those days. These impressive stones, according to Harriette M. Forbes's definitive *Gravestones of Early New England* (1927), were the work of Jonathan and Moses Worster, father and son, who lived and worked in Harvard, providing gravestones to many surrounding towns.

Later in the century another townsman must have taken over the hammer and chisel, for the design of the gravestones changed distinctly. The death's head at the top of the stone became instead the chubby-faced, winged cherub characteristic of New England gravestones of the time; the borders were now of slender, entwined leaves and vines; and the stones were often larger with strictly parallel sides. By 1800 the cherub had been replaced at the top of the stone by a more romantic design, a weeping willow bent over a vase or urn; the stones' borders were usually carved to look like classical columns; and the lettering had reverted to block letters, sharp and uniform, instead of script.

The weeping-willow design was the last stylistic variation local slatecarvers made, though. By the middle of the 1800s the use of slate as a material for gravestones was going out of style, to be replaced by marble and granite. The demise of slate seemed to correspond with the advent of the railroad, which could economically and quickly carry the massive marble and granite from distant quarries. The use of these two stones also led to the end of the slate industry in Harvard; Isaac Stone worked the last quarry on Pin Hill until 1863. By the 1890s Nourse could write, "The portions of the ground earliest occupied, thickly set with low memorials of native slate, in simplicity present an eloquent contrast to the newer lots, loaded with costly obelisks or elaborate monuments of imported marbles and polished granite."

The gravestones at the Center Cemetery tell about much more than just the various artistic styles of local stonecarvers, though. One gravestone inscription succinctly describes the kind of sacrifice the town made to the cause of the Revolution:

> *Here lies ye body*
> *of Andrew Park son of Mr.*
> *John Park and Mrs. Jean Park who*
> *departed this life July 6*
> *1775 in his Country's*
> *service Aged 18 years*
> *1 month and 17 days.*

Some groups of stones—like those of the Cole family, four of whose members died of dysentery within two months—testify to the terrible scourge of epidemic diseases in colonial Harvard.

Another unusual sort of gravemarker was reserved only for a few. The graves of two early ministers, Ebenezer Grosvenor and Daniel Johnson, as well as that of Peter Atherton, are covered with large, rectangular slabs of slate resting on pillars of brick. The long inscriptions on these slabs, litanies of the numerous qualities of the deceased, must have tried the patience of even the most dedicated stonecarver.

Standing by itself in the extreme northwest corner of the cemetery, no closer than twenty-five feet to any other stone in the otherwise crowded graveyard, one stone is an eloquent symbol of the status of Harvard's earliest black residents. The small, undecorated slate marker reads:

> *OTHELLO*
> *The faithful friend of*
> *HENRY BROMFIELD, Came from Africa*
> *about 1760, died 1818,*
> *Aged about 72.*

"Thurlo," as Othello was locally known, was in Nourse's words "an eccentric character, as well known in Harvard as his master." Though given his freedom by Bromfield, Othello chose to remain with and serve the old man; he shadowed the majestic red-cloaked colonel by about ten feet as they walked down the avenue of elms to meeting, and served as master of revels with his fiddle when the Bromfield mansion hosted its famous parties. Henry Bromfield depended on him for companionship throughout his lonely retirement years; and even after Othello's death, the old gentleman would often rise to summon him loudly from the front porch.

Othello was one of perhaps twelve blacks who served as slaves for Harvard's more prosperous white residents during the second half of the eighteenth century. The institution of slavery was apparently not a very popular one in town, though; many of these "servants for life," as they were then called, were freed after serving out contracts such as the one Thomas Wheeler made with his slave:

HARVARD, August 21, 1744.

This may Certifie that Ceasar my Servant is to have his time and be freed from me and any under me at the time of the expiration of four years from the date hereof, if he serves me faithfully till then.
EBENEZER DAVIS   *Witness my hand, THOS. WHEELER.*
JOHN WETHERBEE JUNr.

"An equally noted colored citizen," wrote Nourse, "but one whose life was passed in less aristocratic society, was Cyprian, who figured at the rustic dances, and figures in the town records as 'Sip.' He was the slave of Ephraim Robbins, and apparently, after years of service had impaired his usefulness as a drudge, was granted the cheap boon of freedom. He built for himself a lodging-place, half cellar, half hut, in a lonely hollow in Shabikin, still referred to in deeds as 'Sip's hole,' and kept body and soul together by trapping, fishing, and other ways best known to Cyprian. In time his remnant of strength failed him, and in July, 1768, the town was called upon by Isaac Willard to pay for care rendered and food furnished him. At a later town-meeting Ephraim Robbins was duly notified to excuse himself for his abandonment of this worn-out chattel. Ephraim's statement, if any was made, is not found, but the selectmen were instructed to 'proceed Discressionary in Regard to said Sip.' The poor negro had one prized possession, which he clung to until he saw death near at hand. Like Thurlo, he was a born fiddler, and had furnished the musical inspiration and called the dance figures for all the rural junketings in his neighborhood. His only treasure was an old violin, and this, just before he died—over ninety years of age, in 1784—he had broken into small pieces in his presence, declaring that there should be no 'quarreling over his estate after he was gone.' "

—*Larry Anderson*

6
DIVERSITY AND INDUSTRY

During the new nation's first three decades, the town and townspeople of Harvard underwent changes at an ever increasing rate; these changes were in the direction of greater diversity and fragmentation, of decreased unity and harmony.

In the early years of the 1790s, a number of pedestrian but significant changes were made in the way the town conducted its business, all in the direction of administrative and financial efficiency. In 1790 Harvard was carved up into eight school districts of approximately equal size (see map, page 76). A school committee of eight (one from each district) was elected annually thereafter; a schoolhouse was provided in each district (the center and one or two other districts already had schoolhouses; new structures were built in the remaining districts), and each district had its schoolteacher. Every year at the April meeting each school committeeman reported on receipts and expenditures in his district. The method of apportioning funds to each is not certain, but it was definitely not proportional to the number of students, for an attempt to institute this method of financing the schools was rejected.

In the same year (1790) the town finally settled upon a method for collecting taxes, and ended the annual charade of

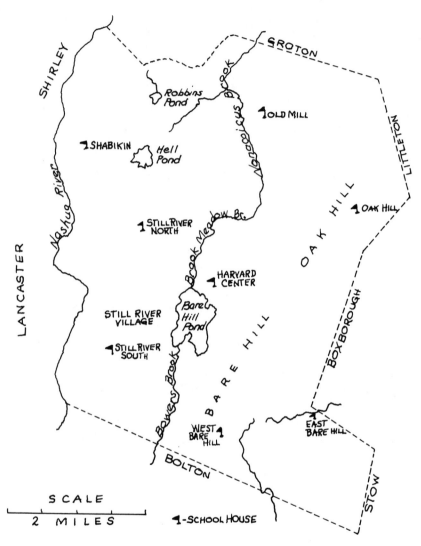

SHIRLEY

GROTON

Robbins Pond

↑ OLD MILL

Noacoicus Brook

↑ SHABIKIN

Hell Pond

LITTLETON

Nashua River

↑ STILL RIVER NORTH

Brook Meadow Br.

OAK HILL

↑ OAK HILL

LANCASTER

↑ HARVARD CENTER

STILL RIVER VILLAGE

Bare Hill Pond

↑ STILL RIVER SOUTH

BARE HILL

BOXBOROUGH

Bowers Brook

WEST BARE HILL ↑

EAST BARE HILL

STOW

BOLTON

SCALE

2 MILES

↑-SCHOOL HOUSE

In 1790 Harvard was carved into eight school districts of approximately equal size. This map does not show the Shaker school district, established in 1816.

electing ten or a dozen constables in order to get one to serve. By paying ten dollars into the town treasury, any person could be relieved of the duties of constable. The town then let out the position of tax collector to the lowest bidder. Someone would offer to collect the town's taxes, usually for a fee of about $30; this person would have to supply two bondsmen who would ensure that the collector carried out his duties faithfully. The collector was then made constable.

This system appears to have been quite successful, for only once in thirty years was there a dispute over tax collection. Captain Oliver Hill had been hired as the tax collector a number of times in the early 1800s; in November 1808 he asked the town for additional compensation for his tax-collecting efforts in 1806, but the town refused this request. Early in 1809 Captain Hill brought suit against the town, and a committee was appointed to marshall a defense. The committee soon found that in 1801 Hill had collected more taxes than had been assessed, and he was ordered to repay to the town this "overplus."

A third change in the town's administrative operation occurred in 1795. Previous to that year all claims on the town's funds had been considered individually by the entire town assembled in meeting. This had apparently become too burdensome and time-consuming, for in 1795 a new policy was instituted whereby most accounts would be considered separately and acted on by the selectmen; the selectmen would then present a summary of their financial transactions as the first item of business at the annual March meeting, immediately preceding the election of new town officers. This report of the selectmen dealt principally with expenditures for the poor, for schools, and for compensation to individuals conducting town business.

In 1792, after the pulpit had been vacant for three years, the town and the church invited the Reverend William Emerson to be their minister, and he accepted. A 1789 graduate of Harvard College, he was a son of William Emerson, who in the years just before the Revolution had been minister at Concord and had on occasion come to Harvard. The younger William was a man of great intellectual powers, whose aspirations were not confined by Harvard's boundaries. His theology was not that of an orthodox Congregational minister, and was labeled "Arminian" by his opponents. "Arminianism" at that time described those persons who adhered to the doctrines of the Unitarian church, and it cannot be doubted that William Emerson sowed many of the seeds that would result, more than two decades later, in the division of the Congregational church in two—the Unitarian and the Evangelical Congregational churches.

The Reverend Mr. Emerson did not limit his intellectual efforts to theological matters. Soon after his arrival in town, he established the first library in Harvard—probably a few books kept in his own parlor and loaned to interested members of his congregation. This first library ceased to function upon Emerson's departure in 1799, but resurfaced a few years later as the Social Library, a subscription library which led a precarious existence until the founding of the free public library in 1856.

In 1799 the First Church of Boston expressed an interest in hiring Mr. Emerson, and he in working for them. After protracted negotiations, Emerson was dismissed from his position at Harvard so that he might become minister of the Boston church; in return, the First Church of Boston gave to the town and church of Harvard a gift of $1,000. This sum of money became the "ministerial fund"; the fund was loaned out in small amounts to a dozen or so townsmen, and the interest derived from these loans was applied to the support of the Congregational minister. In later years, when the town and the church became separated completely, and the church itself split, control over this ministerial fund became a major bone of contention.

Upon his departure, William Emerson commented upon the difficulties of ministering to a congregation afflicted by so much religious dissension. To a certain extent, his remarks harked back to the scandal surrounding John Seccomb, to the strange doings of Shadrach Ireland, and to the beginnings of the Baptists and Shakers in the Revolutionary period. But during Emerson's tenure at Harvard the religious community had shown further signs of fragmentation. Both the Baptists and the Shakers had grown in strength in the 1790s, thereby narrowing the support for the Congregational church. In 1799, the very year of

Emerson's removal, several members of the Congregational church were dismissed to the Methodist church, which was then forming with members from Harvard and Boxborough. In 1804 Dr. Isaiah Parker, founder of the Still River Baptist church, announced his conversion to the Universalist faith, but we may surmise that the conversion had come some years earlier, since he had left his post as Baptist minister in 1798. Thus, by the turn of the century there were in Harvard five religious societies—Congregational, Baptist, Shaker, Methodist, and Universalist.

The establishment of these new churches had weakened the Congregational church by diminishing the number of communicants, but the church was still supported to some extent by the state. The original charter incorporating the town had enjoined the townspeople of Harvard to settle a learned and orthodox minister, and to erect a meetinghouse that would be used as a place of public worship. When the charter was drawn up in 1732, there were no churches competing with the Congregational, and the intermingling of town and church business was accepted as a natural state of affairs. Thus, ever since the founding of Harvard, town meetings had been called to participate in the selection of ministers; and every year the minister's salary was paid by an assessment, voted at town meeting, and collected from all inhabitants who paid rates for non-ecclesiastical purposes.

As new religious sects multiplied and flourished in the closing decades of the nineteenth century, the adherents of various non-Congregational sects became dissatisfied with this system; each sect relied solely on its own members for the funds necessary for the support of a minister and for erecting a house of worship, but at the same time had to contribute financially to the support of the Congregational church. In a sense the members of these recently formed churches were in the same situation as were the people who established Harvard in 1732. Both of these groups were in the position of supporting two churches financially, but reaping (and desiring) the spiritual benefits of only one. The inhabitants of the remote parts of Lancaster, Groton, and Stow in the late 1720s were faced with a geographical problem, and the solution was the formation of a new town. The problem of the religious sectarians of the 1790s was ideological rather than geographical, and a different solution was required.

The first step toward that solution was taken in 1800, when the Shakers petitioned the town for permission to be excluded from assessment for the minister's salary for that year. This petition was referred to the treasurer and assessors, who reported that it was unconstitutional to tax the Shakers for this purpose. A few years later some Harvard townspeople conceived the idea of procuring a bell for calling the Congregational church members to worship on the Sabbath. This required a private subscription for the purchase of the bell, and a town appropriation for the addition of a belltower and steeple to the meetinghouse. Work proceeded on the construction of the steeple in 1806 and was completed in 1807. But the members of other churches than the Congregational were not pleased, and asked to be excused from the expenses of this project, since they felt that the steeple and bell were procured principally for the benefit of the Congregational church. At first the requests of the sectarians were rebuffed; but in March the Shakers were excused from making contributions for the steeple, and in April a similar dispensation was given to the Baptists and Methodists. At the same time a proposal was made to construct a new "town's house," to be used solely for the conduct of town business, as distinct from church business; but this proposal died. These small steps toward complete separation of church and state foreshadowed the climactic events of a decade later, which will be discussed in the next chapter.

During these years when the town was taking a few halting steps toward "modernization" of ecclesiastical affairs, the economic structure of the town was also showing signs of becoming somewhat more open and diversified. In 1794 a survey of Harvard was carried out under state auspices; a glance at this map shows a surprising number of mills scattered around the town, with a concentration of mills on a short stretch of Bowers Brook just north of Pin Hill. Of course every town in New England had a few grist mills and saw mills for local use, but by the mid-1790s we begin to find a number of mills producing materials which could not be completely consumed locally. There was a paper mill, a fulling mill, and, in the Old Mill district near the site of the Jonas Prescott mill of the late 1660s, an iron bloomery that had been operating intermittently since Revolutionary times.

Another new feature of these years around the turn of the century was the emergence of a number of private entrepreneurial ventures, most of them revolving around Colonel Henry Bromfield. In the late 1780s Colonel Bromfield and a few similarly minded men became convinced that there was silver in Oak Hill, and organized a mining operation. This venture lingered on for about four or five years, producing a large hole that can still be seen in the south slope of Oak Hill, but no great amount of silver.

Facing east to Still River from Lancaster's Harvard Road. (Photo by James Macdonald, courtesy Lancaster Historical Commission)

In 1796 a few men living near the center (not including Colonel Bromfield) obtained permission to dig up the Common, in order to lay water pipes from a spring on Bromfield's land to their houses on the Common. This project was quickly consummated and the Harvard Aqueduct was in operation, the forerunner of the present water system.

Colonel Bromfield was again at work in the early 1800s, this time on a projected turnpike through the middle of Harvard. A proposal was floated at a town meeting late in 1804 that Harvard build a section of road that would run to an inn in Leominster, constituting a link in the principal highway from Boston to Albany and other points to the west. The town chose to ignore the issue in 1804, but in 1805 the Bromfield group obtained the approval of the town, and the Union Turnpike was put into operation. The Union Turnpike was very quickly superseded by a better route through Lancaster, but managed to maintain a shadowy existence into the 1820s. Madigan Lane was once a part of the turnpike; if one were to walk due west from the junction of Madigan Lane and Prospect Hill Road, down the slope of Prospect Hill and across the railroad tracks, one would find in the swampy lowlands near the Nashua a raised causeway that was for two decades a part of the turnpike, but is now in sad disrepair.

These changes in the town's economy, small as they were, undoubtedly increased Harvard's contact with the outside world, and brought more travelers through the town than in years past. This increased number of visitors may well be the explanation for the burst of civic pride that resulted in the 1804 regulation that swine *not* be allowed to run at large for the ensuing year. For seventy-two years the last article to be considered at the annual March meeting had been the question of whether or not to allow the swine to run at large, and for seventy-two years the answer had been yes. Finally in 1804 this practice was stopped; all swine, horses, and cattle henceforth were to be maintained within fenced pastures, and could not seek their food on the town's Common and highways. Only once was an exception made; in 1815 the widow Elizabeth Daby was given permission to let her cow free to forage on the Common.

Early in 1801 the town moved to fill the ministerial vacancy created by the departure of William Emerson: Stephen Bemis, a 1798 graduate of Dartmouth, was given the call, accepted, and was ordained on June 3, 1801. In his letter of acceptance Bemis made note of the religious divisions existing in the town, but accepted in spite of them. He also set limits on his own activities, pleading ill health and stating that he would not make as many pastoral visits as his congregation might be accustomed to.

Despite his protestations of ill health, the Reverend Bemis's pastorate was the longest since that of John Seccomb, the town's first Congregational minister. Seccomb had been minister for almost twenty-five years, and since that time no one had lasted for even ten years. Bemis, of course, ministered through a period when the various sects were gaining strength, and no doubt was a participant in the battles over payment of the minister's rate and the assessment for the belltower construction. These conflicts could only have intensified his initial misgivings about the religious differences that already existed in Harvard on his arrival. His crisis and downfall were brought on by the events surrounding the War of 1812.

Harvard responded as it always did to a national military alarm. Provisions were made for paying bounties to Harvard militiamen who went on active duty; resolutions were drafted supporting the national government and its policies; money was appropriated to increase the town stock of gunpowder (the powderhouse that now stands just west of the town hall was built in 1812 to house this new supply of powder).

A national day of fasting and humiliation was called on August 20, 1812, and Mr. Bemis ill-advisedly took that opportunity to preach a sermon in opposition to the war and the actions of the federal government. A large proportion of Harvard's townspeople, including many of Bemis's own congregation, were enraged by this speech, and on August 31 a town meeting was called to discuss the matter. The supporters of the

Reverend Bemis attempted to pass a resolution proclaiming the constitutional right of free speech, without naming the minister or mentioning the issue of the antiwar sermon. This resolution was voted down, 73 for and 88 against. The opposition then introduced a resolution supporting the military measures of the United States government and attacking those who would oppose the war, including the clergy. This resolution passed, although the precise numbers of the votes were not recorded.

This was not the end of the matter, however; at the town meeting of November 12, 1812, called routinely for choosing presidential electors, an article was added to the warrant asking for Mr. Bemis's dismissal. Bemis's supporters were able to head off action at that meeting and obtained an adjournment until the fourth Monday of July 1813, probably hoping that all would be forgotten by then. But Bemis's opponents did not forget, and were able to force a special town meeting on January 18, 1813. The anti-Bemis faction first presented a resolution which allowed those present to express their opinions about Mr. Bemis's antiwar sermon; when opinions were expressed, 72 were against and 45 in favor. At this point Bemis threw in the towel, asking that an ecclesiastical council be called to arrange for his dismissal, and offering to stay on until June, so that a replacement could be found.

The ecclesiastical council was held on June 13, 1813. In his address to that body, Mr. Bemis complained bitterly and at length of the problem of religious division and dissidence in Harvard, and spoke also of his chronic ill health. The counsil voted to dismiss him from his ministerial post, and the Reverend Bemis's days as a preacher were over. Like the Reverend Joseph Wheeler before him, Stephen Bemis remained in town until his death in 1828, working on his farm and taking some interest in town affairs. He was still called the Reverend Bemis after his dismissal.

In late November 1813 the town and the Congregational church joined forces and called Mr. Warren Fay to be their minister. Mr. Fay had graduated from Harvard College in 1807, and had then spent a short time as minister at Brimfield, Massa-

The Shaker schoolhouse. (Courtesy Fruitlands Museums)

chusetts. This would be the last time that the town participated in procuring a minister for the Congregational church, and Mr. Fay would be the last minister to preside over the undivided church. He was ordained in Harvard on January 26, 1814.

The years from 1813 to 1819 were relatively free of religious controversies, but other significant issues arose to fill the void. The Shakers continued their struggle for independence, this time in the field of education. For years they had wanted to establish their own school district, so that their children might be educated in their own ways. Starting in 1809, the Shakers managed to get an article on nearly every town meeting warrant, sometimes three or four times a year, asking that they be designated a separate school district. Every time they were rejected, except for one occasion in 1813 when the town acceded to their wishes, and then immediately reversed the vote. Finally in 1816 the Shakers decided to seek help from a higher authority, and petitioned the General Court for assistance. This apparently frightened the opposition, for a deal was quickly arranged whereby the Shakers would withdraw their petition in return for being admitted as a new school district on equal footing with the older districts. This agreement was formalized on November 4, 1816, and from that day there were nine school districts in Harvard.

In 1819 the town transferred some of the decision-making authority on school matters from the selectmen to the individual districts. The districts were organized as semi-independent authorities, each one having a clerk and a moderator; the latter was usually the district's school committeeman. Each district would meet in its own public meeting, passing on various school expenditures and on the choice of a schoolmaster.

At about the same time the town adopted a more efficient method of dealing with the poor. Since the 1790s the number of poor had been increasing steadily, and the institution of "vendueing the poor" had arisen. The "vendue" was an annual auction at which individuals would bid to support one or more of the town's poor. The lowest bidder would undertake to provide for a poverty-stricken person or family for a year, and the town would pay the bill. From time to time attempts had been made to improve on this system, but not until 1817 was a committee chosen to investigate the problem. On March 2, 1818 the committee recommended that the care of the poor should be let out to one person, and for a period of more than one year. This new recommendation was immediately put into effect, the low bidder being Captain Oliver Hill, who agreed to supervise the town's poor for three years for $2,500. The same Captain Hill ten years earlier had clashed with the town over his accounts as tax collector.

At this same town meeting the Universalist Society asked that it be allowed to use the meetinghouse each year for a number of Sabbaths proportional to the fraction of the minister's rate paid by Universalist members in that year. This proposal was rejected, but the incident signalled the re-emergence of religious controversy in Harvard, and may be seen as the first skirmish in a long and complicated battle that would end a few years later with the town and church completely separated, and with the Congregational church itself split into two nearly equal parts.

§ Harvard Publications

Sometime around the year 1800, two Harvard brothers, Luther and Sewall Parker, established the first commercial printing shop in Harvard. Working from their shop in the north part of Still River, they probably did the sort of job printing—posters, business forms, and the like—that small printers have always done. But the Parker brothers were also probably the first in a long string of Harvard people— entrepreneurs, eccentrics, and students—to produce native Harvard publications.

For at least the years 1806 through 1811 the Parker brothers printed and sold an almanac, *Trufant's Family Almanac and Daily Register*, which they claimed was "Fitted to the Latitude and Longitude of BOSTON, (Mass.) and to serve for all the adjoining states." Like any other farmer's almanac, the Parkers' was filled with "a large quantity and great variety of other matter, NEW, USEFUL, INSTRUCTIVE & ENTERTAINING," such as astronomical and astrological information and calculations; a running weather forecast; schedules and routes of stage coach lines; holiday and court calendars; medical, legal, and agricultural advice; and all sorts of aphorisms and admonitions along the line of those popularized in Benjamin Franklin's *Poor Richard's Almanac*.

According to Henry Nourse's town history, the person after whom the almanac was named and who probably compiled it was one Joseph Trufant, who "resided for a time in Harvard, having come thither from Groton in 1800." Trufant and the Parkers did indeed put out an "instructive and useful" publication, but much of the material found in it seems to have been extracted, perhaps even plagiarized, from other popular journals and almanacs of the day. One entry in the 1810 edition was "The Farmer's Calendar, by the Moon":

"Cut timber for duration, Last Quarter. Posts for the ground in the new. Firewood, in the First Quarter. Cut hedges between the new and full. Graft and plant trees in the new. Kill cattle or swine at the full. Alter cattle from the last Quarter, to the new, when the sign is in the *head, thighs, or knees.* Shear sheep, if they loose wool, in the old; otherwise in the new. Gather Apples, Pears &c. at the full. Manure lands, to prevent weeds, in the last Quarter. Sow Flax at the Apogee. Gather herbs, flowers, or seeds, at the full."

In the 1811 edition, possibly the last, more space is given over to humor and poetry and there is a little less of the practical information that marked the previous year's almanac. Perhaps the quality of the humor in the 1811 edition explains the demise of the almanac—Nourse reports that the Parkers stayed in business only about ten years and that Luther moved to Michigan and Sewall to New York. Under the heading "Anecdotes" is included the entry:

"A young man, lately made a Justice of the peace, was asked by another, what would be done with a man who committed suicide? The squire, with much majesterial gravity, answered, that 'he must be confined in the state prison, to hard labor, during life.' "

The Harvard Shakers operated a printing press for a period of time in the early 1800s, probably producing many of their own religious tracts. But the most interesting publication to come off their press was a weekly periodical called "Something New," published in the 1830s. In this little magazine a non-Shaker, Michael H. Barton, attempted to promote a phonetic alphabet that could, he claimed, be universally used and understood. Barton had published his weekly, apparently without much success, in Exeter, New Hampshire and Boston before Harvard's Shaker printers took on the job; perhaps they were impressed with Barton's seemingly progressive system of writing and were willing to help him promote it.

The purpose of this system, Barton wrote, was "to improve and perfect the orthography of the English language by substituting an alphabet in place of the present one which shall contain thirty-nine letters, each representing one of the distinct sounds used in our language."

His new alphabet resembles shorthand writing and is virtually incomprehensible; indeed, it must have been extremely difficult to set into type. As it turned out, "Something New" ceased publication after only a few years.

Another twenty years passed before any more attempts were made to publish a Harvard-based periodical—and the ones that turn up for the 1850s and 1860s are purely amateur efforts. In fact these handwritten newspapers, with names like the "Harvard Weekly

Journal," the "Experiment," and the "Independent," seem to have been written and edited for the most part by bright and enterprising Harvard teenagers. None of these young publishers lasted very long, apparently; the little papers collected at the Harvard Historical Society cease after Volume I, Number 6.

A shortage of material, the tedious labor of writing out by hand each ten- or twelve-page copy, and a high price perhaps explain why none of these papers lasted very long—unless their demise can be attributed to the simple fact that young editors and publishers soon grew out of their early enthusiasm for seeing their work in print. The "editresses" of the Harvard Weekly Journal, Fannie Willard and O. J. Reed, charged $6.00 a year for their paper, which only came out ten times over that period—though "Clergymen, Schoolteachers and Postmasters, can be supplied with the Journal at half the usual price." In the editorial of their third edition they are "hoping to be able to thank contributors for their munificence in furnishing matter for our papers, but we have waited in vain and shall be obliged to turn our intended thanks into complaints for the withholding of such help." The town's juvenile newspapers did not last long.

Along with Henry S. Nourse, whose history of the town was published by Warren Hapgood in 1894, one of the better known chroniclers of Harvard life was Frederick S. Savage, who lived in Still River at the turn of the century and who, on his own, published two books. The first of these, *Memoirs of Old Harvard Days, from 1863 to 1924*, published in 1924, was a collection of articles Savage had written over the years for Turner's Public Spirit of Ayer. In these forty-four letters to the Public Spirit (which in those days also came out with a local edition, the Harvard Hillside) Savage describes just about everyone he had ever known in the town of Harvard. Of his omniscience about the people and activities of Harvard, Savage wrote, "In regard to knowing so many people in Town, I will say that in the late sixties and early seventies there was not one family in Town but I knew them or of them, for at that time everyone in Town came to the center for their mail, and also at that time most everyone in Town went to Church each Sunday and listened to two sermons. Also in my younger days there was no road in Town but I had traveled over it some time or another. Hence my knowledge of each farm and home."

In 1931 Savage produced a short, but more personal book, *Wood Pile Chips: Poetry, Poems, and Letters.* This book came out when he was 72 years old, and Mr. Savage, a man of strong opinions, was not afraid to let people know what he thought.

One of the problems Savage was most concerned about was Prohibition, which he vehemently opposed. In his essay, "The

Eighteenth Amendment," he writes, "If the United States Government was building an up to date College to educate high class criminals, then the 18th Amendment to the Constitution has surely accomplished its purpose." He continues, "Now I will say something and I am quite sure it will come true, and that is, if the Republican Party, of which I am a life long member, want to carry the Election this year, and also our next Presidential Election, they must elect men that have courage of their convictions, that are ringing wet, so one can see the whiskey dropping out of their coat tails; I do not mean drunkards, but strong men that are sober—but are wise enough to see that the 18th Amendment is not a success and must be removed from the laws of this country. . . . Some of the readers of this article may think I am a Socialist or a Nihilist, but I am neither; I am a member of the Congregational Church, I fear God only, and do try to live right."

Many other publications have either been produced in Harvard or describe events that have taken place in town over the years. Louisa May Alcott's story "Transcendental Wild Oats," published first in the *Independent* in 1873 and then reprinted in 1876 in the collection called *Silver Pitchers*, is a dramatized and humorous account of the Fruitlands experiment. Miss Alcott was a child of ten during the year her father tried and failed to establish a utopian community on the western slope of Prospect Hill. Written some thirty years after the Alcotts' year in Harvard, "Transcendental Wild Oats" is perhaps the best record of this small but important chapter in Harvard's history.

From 1921 until 1933 Fiske Warren published an annual book called *Enclaves of Economic Rent*. Updated from year to year, these books contain descriptions not just of the Tahanto and Shakerton enclaves, but also of the other single tax communities throughout the United States and the rest of the world. Filled with sample legal documents and the financial accountings of each single tax community, these books do not make for very interesting reading; but they are the most reliable source for information about the development and operation of the various single tax enclaves.

In September 1973 Edward Miller and Kathleen Cushman established the Harvard Post, the town's first full-fledged weekly newspaper. Besides covering the normal range of current town affairs, the newspaper has regularly published a variety of articles of historical interest, including reports on a number of local events and institutions and interviews with some of Harvard's older residents.

—Larry Anderson

7

THE STRUGGLE
FOR PERFECTION

In mid-1819 the Reverend Mr. Warren Fay, the seventh minister of the First Church of Harvard, asked that he be dismissed from his pastoral position. Like a number of his predecessors, he cited recurrent religious bickering, and claimed that it was impossible to preside over a divided congregation. The ritual ecclesiastical council was called, and again the town of Harvard was without a settled minister. But this time there was a difference. The multiplying sects and the increasing split between church and state had weakened the position of the Congregational church; even more damaging was the split within the Congregational church itself.

Harvard's long string of ministers had held and propounded a wide variety of theological doctrines, and various segments of the Harvard congregation had been affected in different ways. Some remembered the days of William Emerson's ministry, and were still under the influence of his "Arminian" views. Another group, perhaps not quite so large as the first, was more in sympathy with the recently departed Mr. Fay, who espoused a more orthodox and evangelical form of Calvinism.

In spite of these difficulties, some members of the church attempted to proceed as in the past, and the usual committees

This early engine of the Worcester & Nashua railroad line bore the name "Harvard." (Courtesy Harvard Historical Society)

were selected—one to supply the pulpit temporarily, and another to search for a permanent occupant. This time, though, progress was slow; the opposing factions could not agree on a suitable minister. To make matters worse, the town in 1820 refused for the first time in its existence to appropriate money for the minister's salary. This left the members of the Congregational church in a sad state indeed; once these ties with the town had been sundered, they had no legal means of raising money for support of a minister, or performing those other corporate acts that were routine as long as the church functioned within the limits of the town's charter.

It became necessary therefore for the newly independent Congregational church to incorporate itself as a separate parish. Under these circumstances the developing factionalism within the church became dominant, and the first side to take action was the group who identified most closely with the Reverend Warren Fay. This group, led by Salmon Whitney, Jonathan Beard, and John Hapgood, seized the initiative on New Year's Day, 1821. On that day a "town meeting" was held (apparently attended only by members of this one faction) at which it was decided to petition the General Court for a charter as an independent parish, and for full use of the meetinghouse and the ministerial fund.

Only a week later, on January 8, the opposition, whose leaders included the long since deposed Reverend Bemis, itself held a "town meeting" at which was read a remonstrance against the meeting of January 1. This remonstrance claimed that the Whitney-Beard-Hapgood group did not represent real Congregationalism, was a minority of the pewholders, and should not have control of the meetinghouse and ministerial fund.

The General Court sided with the latter group, and the heirs of William Emerson's teachings continued their existence as the First Congregational Church in Harvard, now the Unitarian church. The members were soon organized as the First Parish. They had the use of the meetinghouse, but the ministerial fund was left in the hands of a group of disinterested trustees, and was not used for the support of the Unitarian church until 1838. The

The Still River Depot. (Courtesy Harvard Historical Society)

First Parish, or Unitarian Society, invited Ira Henry Thomas Blanchard to fill the pulpit on a temporary basis, but was so pleased with his performance that he was asked to be the first minister of the reorganized church. He was ordained on January 1, 1823 and served until April 13, 1831.

The Whitney-Beard-Hapgood group, having lost in its attempt to become the successor of the original Congregational church, soon declared itself to be a new and independent church, and was known as the Evangelical or Calvinistic Congregational Church. Their first meeting was held on March 14, 1821; they soon had a constitution, but needed a meetinghouse. They applied to the town for a grant of land on the Common for a place to erect a church; this petition was acted upon at the town meeting of May 7, 1821, when the Calvinistic Congregational Church was given the tract of land where its church now stands. A few days later the church society invited George Fisher to be minister; on September 12 he was ordained in the nearly finished meetinghouse, and the Calvinistic Congregational Church was firmly established. The Reverend Fisher's ministry was long by Harvard standards; he died in office on September 6, 1853, after thirty-two years of service.

The split between church and town had left the meetinghouse in the hands of the Unitarian Society. The town now had no place to meet that could be called the "town's house." Harvard struggled along for several years, meeting sometimes at the center schoolhouse, and sometimes at Mr. Wetherbee's tavern on the east side of the Common, but usually at the old Congregational (now Unitarian) meetinghouse. Finally, on August 27, 1827, a committee was appointed to study the problem of finding a permanent building for the transaction of town business. At first the committee claimed that the old Congregational meetinghouse belonged to the town; but previous state supreme court rulings in similar cases in other towns had always gone in favor of the church society of those towns. The committee then presented plans for a new town's house to be built for $700. The plans were at first rejected, but necessity soon forced the townspeople to accept them, and by November 1828 the "town house" was in use. (Not until 1832 was the term "town hall" used to describe this building.) This first town hall was on the east side of Ayer Road, approximately opposite the present town hall, and served the town for nearly forty years.

The town hall was not used for town business only; in 1837 the town granted "the use of the Town Hall for Lectures on Moral Scientific Religious and Political subjects generally, provided nevertheless the Hall shall not be used for the discussion of any subject affecting the right of domestick Slavery in the United States, in any form whatever." Two years later the restriction on discussions of slavery was lifted.

No doubt one of the lecture subjects in those days was the evils of alcohol. The earliest temperance societies in Harvard were active in the 1820s, 1830s, and 1840s. Various groups (one under the sobering name of the "Young Men's Total Abstinence Society and Cold Water Army") met frequently so that the members might receive one another's encouragement. Zophar Wetherbee, the town's principal innkeeper and purveyor of distilled and other spirits, was convinced (for the price of $400) to cease the sale of rum, and Wetherbee's Tavern—long a major stopping-point on the stagecoach route to Worcester—was known for a time as Wetherbee's Temperance Hotel. As these temperance societies temporarily achieved their objectives, participation in the group meetings dropped off and the societies faded away.

The problem of alcohol was also on the minds of the men who cared for the town's poor. The experiment begun in 1818, under which Captain Oliver Hill was paid one sum of money annually to care for the poor, was discontinued after one three-year term. The town returned to the older practice of "vendueing" or auctioning off the poor to the lowest bidder. This did not prove to be any more successful than in years past, and in September 1823 a committee was solemnly chosen to study why pauperism was on the increase and what were its causes. The committee, which included Captain Hill, deliberated for thirty minutes, and returned with a report that pauperism was caused by the excessive consumption of alcoholic beverages. It recommended that the sale of alcohol be restricted, and that intoxicating beverages no longer be provided at funerals.

TEMPERANCE

FESTIVAL,

FEBRUARY 22, 1849,

BY THE

HARVARD

TEMPERANCE SOCIETIES.

Mr. Ephⁿ Abbot and Family, are invited to the Anniversary meeting, at L. Wetherbee's Hotel, on Thursday, the 22 inst., at 4 o'clock, P. M.

Distinguished Speakers are expected to be present on that occasion.

Tickets 50 cts. Children under 12 years, 25 cts. Supper at 5 1-2 o'clock.

Harvard,
Feb. 8, 1849.

Luke Pollard, Jr.
H. M. Smart,
S. W. Rayment,
H. F. Davis,
Jerome Farnsworth,

COMMITTEE.

BROWN'S PRESS, GROTON.

Wetherbee's Temperance Hotel was the scene for annual festivals that drew teetotalers from miles around. (Courtesy Harvard Historical Society)

In April 1825 the town decided to end the practice of vendueing, and voted to buy a farm which would be used to provide
housing and minimal employment for the poor. On June 20,
1825, a committee was provided with $2,400 in order to buy the
96-acre farm of Phineas Davis. The committee soon became
formalized as the Overseers of the Poor, a group which administered the farm and reported to the town annually. A caretaker
was hired to run the farm, and by March 1826 the poor farm was
functioning, and the old method of vendueing became obsolete.

In 1832 Harvard celebrated its centennial, and a year later
the centennial of the organization of the Congregational church
in Harvard. On each of these occasions, the Reverend George
Fisher, minister of the Calvinistic Congregational Church,
delivered a historical address. These orations were largely cata-
logues of town and church officers, and summaries of the
numbers of baptisms, marriages, and burials under each minister. The Reverend Fisher did, however, make a few penetrating
observations; the following is taken from his sermon on town
history:

> It is probable, that during the first half of the Century, the
> population of the town rapidly increased. Its increase, during the
> last forty or fifty years, has, however, been comparatively small.
> This has been owing to several causes. The scarcity of Water-
> privileges is one. On this account, but little opportunity for
> engaging in Manufacturing business has been afforded to the
> natives of the town, who have, therefore, in many instances, left
> the town for the purpose of engaging in such business abroad.
> Another of the causes to which I refer, I apprehend to be the fact,
> that but little encouragement has, in many instances, been afford-
> ed to the young men of the town to settle here as cultivators of the
> farms. The inquiry with the landholders has usually seemed to be,
> not into how many farms their land might be divided, and how
> many young families it might be made comfortably to support,
> but how their farms might be increased in size, and how few of
> their sons might be encouraged to remain upon them. One obvious
> and unhappy consequence has been, that very many of the most
> promising young men of the town, who would gladly have lived
> and died here as agriculturalists if they had received sufficient

encouragement, have emigrated to other places, and engaged in other business.

Fisher's portrayal of the town's population growth is accurate: from an initial figure of about 350 in 1732, the population had reached 1,315 by 1776. The population rose slowly thereafter, until in 1830, just two years before the town's centennial, the figure was around 1,600. This level was maintained until mid-century, then began to slowly decline. The population of the 1830–1850 period would not again be attained until the "baby boom" following World War II.

The "water-privileges" were concentrated principally along Bowers Brook just north of Pin Hill. Several mill ponds were created on this short stretch of water, and mills were operated at each of these sites throughout the nineteenth century. None of them was successful for any length of time; a good picture of mill operation in Harvard can be obtained from the following excerpt from Nourse, describing the number of times one millsite changed hands in the course of a few decades only.

> The firm of Stacy and Sawyer about 1831 built below the upper dam on the brook a large mill, the basement of which was filled with machinery for the making of wrapping paper, while the upper story was used as a lead-pencil factory. . . . The company became embarrassed, however, and in 1839 assigned their property to John P. Whitcomb and Jerome Gardner for the benefit of their creditors. The mills were sold at auction . . . , John Stacy, Jr., purchasing . . . the paper and pencil factory. Mr. Stacy was compelled to place heavy mortgages upon his property, and in 1859 his creditors sold the upper mills to Mr. Stone. In 1860 Nahum Harwood and Sherman Fletcher bought all Mr. Stone's rights, and by a subsequent agreement Mr. Harwood took the paper-mill, into which was introduced machinery for the making of leather board. . . . In 1866, Mr. Harwood disposed of the upper mill and the water rights to the American Machine Company of Newburyport, the consideration named being $14,000. The next year the mill was again transferred to James Blood, William Graves, William H. Brewster and others for $18,000, and in 1868 the Harvard Manufacturing Company was organized with a capital of $40,000. . . . [T]he company sold to Charles W. S. Adams of Chelmsford its works, known as the Excelsior Mill, and

This mill at the corner of Depot Road and Mill Road saw many owners and produced such goods as leatherboard, paper, pencils, and excelsior. (Courtesy Harvard Historical Society)

the water rights for the sum of $3,000. The mill was closed in August, 1880, and sold by Mr. Adams to Walter S. Watson of Lowell in 1882. It has been temporarily leased by Mr. Watson for the making of shoddy, wool-scouring, etc., but is now idle.

Harvard in the middle decades of the nineteenth century was not a growing and prosperous mill town, as were so many New England towns of that era. Harvard was a stagnant agricultural town, supplying laborers and entrepreneurs to the towns that were becoming manufacturing centers.

With the passing decades the Shaker Society had become routinely accepted by Harvard's townspeople. No longer did riotous mobs descend on Shaker meetings and attempt to drive these sectarians out of town. The Shaker way of life had expanded rapidly in the 1790s and early years of the 1800s, with more than a dozen communities being founded in New England, New York, and Ohio, including a sister community just across the Nashua River in Shirley.

In many ways the Shakers in Harvard (as elsewhere) were a

THE RURAL HOME.

Allow me to respectfully call your attention to the advantages offered by the Rural Home as a refuge from the annoyances of city life and the summer heats. The Rural home is a substantial Brick Building, 90 x 50 ft., three and a half stories high. It was built for a dwelling for a branch of the family of Harvard Shakers, and the continuous and increasing applications from the cities for summer board, induced them to fit it up for that purpose. Its location and surroundings fill all the requirements for

A PERFECT COUNTRY HOME.

It is thirty miles from Boston, by Fitchburg Railroad, and one mile from the Ayer station, on the summit of a gentle rise, with shaded avenues and walks and pleasant drives in every direction, and whatever a farm contributes to make up the pleasure, in contrast with the dust and heat of the city. A more quiet and retired Home cannot be found in the state.

All those desiring perfect freedom from the exacting demands of fashionable customs of dress and society, can here be sure of finding their wants gratified. The appointments of the house are excellent; the halls are wide, the rooms large and airy, twice the size of ordinary hotel rooms, with dressing-rooms attached. A spring supplies the house with pure soft water. The table is supplied with the choicest production of the Shaker Community.

Those who wish to bring their teams will find the best of accommodations and care. There are sixteen trains each way daily, all stopping at Ayer Junction. Special rates for business men can be had by applying to the proprietor, and package and family tickets, with liberal discount, can be obtained at the Boston office, and also at the Home. Carriage to convey passengers to and from the Home on the arrival of the trains.

Those contemplating the quiet and comfort of this "Home" will do well to apply soon to secure their rooms. We invite you to a personal inspection.

Address JOHN H. SPRAGUE, Rural Home, AYER, MASS.

(Courtesy Harvard Historical Society)

self-contained community, almost completely independent of the town's control. After their original acquisition of the Square House and the real estate held by Shadrach Ireland, the Shakers had gone on to purchase many hundreds of acres, to the point where they controlled most of the northeast corner of Harvard. Much of the money for these real estate transactions came from the estates of new converts to the Shaker religion who settled in the Harvard community. In accord with Shaker communal doctrines, new converts had to relinquish all personal possessions to the society, and this wealth became available for use in the Shakers' territorial expansion.

At its point of maximum expansion, the Harvard Society had about two hundred members. Some of these were native Harvard residents, but more were attracted from other towns. Thus, much of Harvard's slight population growth from the time of the Revolution to the time of the Reverend Fisher's centennial sermon may be attributed to the successful expansion of the Shaker community.

These two hundred members of Harvard's Shaker Village were divided into four "families"—the Church or Centre, the North, the South, and the East. Each family had its own farm and dormitory buildings. Each family lived and worked together as a unit; when the Shaker Society was at its peak, all farm work was done by the Shakers themselves, without hired labor. (Later, as the village declined, the Shakers had to bring in hired hands to keep the farms running.) Shaker doctrine required complete celibacy—the faith was to be propagated solely through conversion—and the sexes were separated in every aspect of daily life. Males and females slept in different dormitory rooms, and ate at different tables in the dining room. At times of worship, the major aspect of which was a simple form of group dancing and singing, men and women danced in separate groups on opposite sides of the room.

The first task of the Shakers at Harvard in their growing years was the cultivation and improvement of the tracts of land they had acquired, probably the worst agricultural land in Harvard. They built their own grist mill and saw mill, for use by the whole Shaker community. After they had secured their own agricultural subsistence, they directed their energies toward production of various simple manufactures for sale to the outside world. Different Shaker communities emphasized different products; at Harvard the principal products were brooms, bottled herbs, applesauce, and packaged garden seeds.

The Shakers' industry provided them with a very prosperous and comfortable material life. Although they stressed simplicity, theirs was not a life of austerity and self-denial. They ate well, dressed well, and kept in step with the modern conveniences in kitchen and bathroom plumbing. Education was stressed; for many years they had fought for their own school district, and had at last attained the right to educate the young people of their community in Shaker ways. Magazines and newspapers were taken by the elders of the village, showing that they were not completely cut off from worldly affairs.

Simplicity, industry, communal property—these characteristics are associated with many utopian communities. But what were the religious doctrines peculiar to the Shakers? They

The South Shaker family's stone barn. (Courtesy Fruitlands Museums)

Eldress Josephine leading the Shaker sisters from the meetinghouse on the Sabbath. (Courtesy Fruitlands Museums)

believed that Mother Ann Lee was the Second Christ, and that after her coming, all Believers were living in a heaven on earth. This last point helps explain the separation of sexes; in heaven, they reasoned, there are no sexes. A principal tenet of the Shakers was that with the second coming of Christ in the person of Mother Ann, all men might be redeemed. This was of course contrary to the Calvinistic doctrine of predestination, which divided men into the elect and the damned. This difference of doctrine no doubt contributed to the early animosities between the Shakers and the traditionalist Congregationalists of Harvard; but as the Congregational church underwent divisions and doctrinal disputes, the unusual ideas of the Shakers no longer attracted as much attention, and some of the tensions between Shakers and townspeople were diminished.

In striking contrast to the success of the Shakers is the story of another utopian community which existed in Harvard for a few months in 1843. This community was a brainchild of Amos Bronson Alcott, a friend of Ralph Waldo Emerson and Henry David Thoreau, and father of Louisa May Alcott, author of *Little Women*. Bronson Alcott was active in the intellectual movement known as transcendentalism, and in the years immediately prior to 1843 had been in London attempting to put his advanced educational theories into practice.

In London Alcott had met a number of kindred spirits, among whom was Charles Lane. Probably influenced by Emerson's writings, this little group of idealists conceived of founding the utopian community that they would name Fruitlands. Like the Shaker community, Fruitlands was to be a communal effort; and again like the Shakers, the members of the Fruitlands experiment would attempt to be self-sufficient. But Alcott and his associates went further than the Shakers; they were to be vegetarians, and in fact wished to make no use of animals at all, not even for plowing their fields. Where the Shakers were willing to maintain extensive economic relations with a wider world, the Fruitlands group wished to trade only for essential items they were completely incapable of producing for themselves. The Alcott-Lane experiment did not have any explicit religious or Christian elements, but did stress elevation of the spirit and pursuit of wisdom.

Early in 1843 Alcott and Lane were able to arrange for the purchase of a farm on the west slope of Prospect Hill, overlooking the Nashua River Valley, and the little group of transcendentalists (ten, including children) moved in. A few converts were attracted during the summer of that year, but the number was never very great, and none stayed very long. The Alcott group did not possess the industry or foresight of the Shakers, and was unable to provide itself with enough food and supplies to survive through even one winter. Before the end of the first year the group had dispersed and the experiment ended before it had really begun.

During the few months of Fruitlands' existence, Alcott, Lane, and others made at least one trip to visit the Shakers for an exchange of utopian thoughts. The Fruitlands group thought the Shakers too worldly, and disapproved of their consumption of the flesh of animals. Upon the breakup of Fruitlands, Charles Lane briefly joined the Shakers, before his return to England. Bronson Alcott and his family lived in Harvard for another few months, then moved to Concord to be nearer the intellectual group that suited Alcott best.

In 1848, five years after the failure of Fruitlands, the railroad came to Harvard. In 1845 the Boston and Fitchburg Railway had opened stations in Ayer and Littleton, but this line did not run through Harvard. The Worcester and Nashua Railway did run a line through Harvard, connecting to Groton and Worcester; the tracks ran along the western slope of Prospect Hill, right through the Fruitlands farm. Depots were located at Still River and at the northern end of Prospect Hill, northwest of the center of town. The railroad ensured increased communication and closer contact with the outside world. Many predicted increased prosperity for Harvard, but the true effects of the railroad would not be known for many years.

§ Joseph Palmer's Beard

That the Fruitlands community survived even as long as it did—and that was less than a year—was largely because of the efforts of Joseph Palmer, a farmer from NoTown, a village on the outskirts of Fitchburg; Palmer moved to Fruitlands in July 1843 and supplied the utopian community with its only element of practical knowledge and experience about agriculture.

About two years after Fruitlands was abandoned, Palmer, who in the meantime had returned to his home at NoTown, bought the farm on the western slope of Prospect Hill from Ralph Waldo Emerson. Emerson had been holding the property as trustee for Charles Lane, cofounder of the Consociate Family, and sold it to Palmer for nine hundred dollars. Renaming the farm "Freelands," Palmer lived there for almost thirty more years, during which time he ran the place as a sort of halfway house and hostel for tramps, ex-convicts, and other low characters of all descriptions.

Palmer had a particular reason for empathizing with and helping out such wayfarers. In 1830 Palmer himself had been thrown in the

The earliest photograph of the Fruitlands house. (Courtesy Fruitlands Museums)

Worcester County Jail and kept there for more than a year as a sort of political prisoner. His crime? Wearing a beard.

Palmer, though a successful Yankee farmer, was by no means a typical one. Throughout his life he had been active in religious and reform movements of all sorts—and in the early 1800s such movements abounded in New England. Possibly influenced in childhood by a bearded itinerant evangelist named Lorenzo Dow, Palmer in the 1820s took to wearing a long beard in the face of being considered eccentric and slovenly, beards being very unpopular at that time. Regularly harassed and questioned about his insistence on wearing the beard, Palmer advanced both practical and spiritual arguments to justify his whiskers. To some he cited the absurdity of a man's scraping away at his face every day of the year. A prominent Fitchburg minister once accosted him: "Palmer, why don't you shave and not go around looking like the devil?" Palmer replied, "Mr. Trask, are you not mistaken in your comparison of personages? I have never seen a picture of the ruler of the sulphurous regions with much of a beard, but if I remember correctly, Jesus wore a beard not unlike mine."

One day early in May 1830, at the height of Fitchburg's vexation with Palmer for wearing a beard, four men armed with scissors and razors attacked Palmer outside a Fitchburg hotel and attempted to shave him. Palmer successfully fended off his attackers; he was even able to unloose his jackknife and wound the legs of two of his assailants. Charged with "unprovoked assault," Palmer was arraigned a few days later before Judge David Brigham on that charge. Thus began Palmer's ordeal in the Worcester County Jail for refusing to pay the ten dollar fine, nearly forty dollars in court fees, and the seven hundred dollar bond that resulted from his conviction for the crime of defending his right to wear a beard.

Palmer, a stubborn, intelligent, righteous, and meticulous character, kept a detailed journal of his fifteen months in the jail at Worcester; now preserved at Fruitlands Museums, it records the words and actions of his often sadistic jailers, the experiences of his fellow prisoners, and his own steadfastness in resisting the efforts of the state and society to break him of his unconventional habits and opinions.

Palmer's term in jail was extremely unpleasant at times. He was dangerously sick during his first few weeks behind bars. Later, he was beaten several times by the jailers, nearly starved for days at a time, placed in solitary confinement for several months, and physically threatened by other prisoners who tried to cut off his beard. But Palmer made life nearly as difficult for the officials who were keeping him in the jail as they made it for him. To Calvin Willard, Sheriff of Worcester County, he sent a constant stream of letters, complaining of the poor conditions in the jail, such as the following: "Sir, I have suffered severely on Saturday last by some prisoners in the South Room and was not then releaved by Mr. Bellows [the jailer] although he had information and was requested to do so. I wish you to see them brought to Justice for their outrageous Conduct. yours &c. Joseph Palmer." One time, to prove to the sheriff how little food he was receiving, he sent Willard a package containing every morsel of food the jailers had given him in one day.

For such acts as that, the jailkeepers, especially Hosea Bellows and Dorance Wilder, treated Palmer even worse. On September 22, 1830, after a little more than four months in prison, Palmer exploded in distress and fury at the treatment he and his fellow prisoners were receiving. He paid for his outburst by spending the next three months in solitary confinement.

After Palmer had spent a year in jail, not having budged an inch in his insistence of innocence or in his demands for decent treatment, the jailers had apparently come to grant him a small measure of respect and had reached a sort of truce with the stubborn and proud farmer:

> . . . Mr. & Mrs. Bellows come in with a Man & Woman who had ben at the House over Sunday. Bellows said well Mr. Palmer do you feel any better than you did the other day. I said, I feel about the same as I did. I am pretty much everry day alike about these

days. I cant perceive much difference lately. Bellows said, you are quite a regular sort of a man. I said, yes. I am not wheeled about by every wind and Doctrine. I am stedfast and unmoveable always abounding. Bellows said, yes. yes. I see you are one of those substantial and firm kind of Men. I said, I am glad you begin to find it out. . . . [*Courtesy Fruitlands Museums*]

Throughout his imprisonment Palmer insisted that he was innocent and that to pay a fine, even of only ten dollars, would be to admit his guilt. Palmer became something of an embarrassment to county authorities, who realized that his jail term was far exceeding his "crime," and they sent several committees to the jail to convince him to leave. They would waive the seven hundred dollar bond, they said, if he would only pay the fine and the court fees. Palmer told one of the committees, "If I aint a safe person to have my Liberty I ought not to go out. and I am willing to stay in confinement til I am."

It was not until David Brigham, the judge before whom Palmer had originally appeared, came to Worcester to beg him to leave, that Palmer relented. Brigham also carried a letter from Palmer's mother, a woman well into her eighties, pleading with Palmer to come home. On August 31, 1831, after more than fifteen months of imprisonment for defending his right to wear a beard, Palmer paid his fine and left the jail.

Imprisonment only reinforced Palmer's interest in political and religious reform, though. He was involved in prison reform and was an early abolitionist. In the early 1840s he attended the Chardon Street Convention in Boston which, according to one report, debated "whether the Christian faith is of divine or human origin. Some have called it an infidel convention." It was at this meeting that Palmer met such prominent figures as Emerson, Bronson Alcott, and William Lloyd Garrison.

His acquaintance with Alcott led to his decision to join Fruitlands. From 1846, when he bought the farm after the demise of the utopian experiment, until his death in 1873, Palmer's farm on Prospect Hill was open to every tramp and wayfarer. By the time he was in his sixties the "crime" for which he had suffered, wearing a beard, had become a commonplace, even respectable, habit among American men.

—*Larry Anderson*

8
THE WAR
AND MORE CONSTRUCTION

The decade immediately before the Civil War was a relatively uneventful one in Harvard's history. Religion was no longer so strong a force in people's lives as it had once been, and religious disputes no longer intruded themselves into the town's business. The school system was functioning as it had since the turn of the century, with nine autonomous districts and no high school; private out-of-town academies were the only available intermediaries between the elementary education of the local schoolhouse and the advanced learning of the few New England colleges. The town's highways were still maintained by all the townspeople, "paying" their taxes by doing a few days' work on the roads nearest their farms. These institutions, and others as well, would undergo significant change after the Civil War, but in the years just after mid-century Harvard's public institutions were in a quiescent phase.

The 1850s did, however, witness one institutional advance in Harvard. For fifty years and more a private subscription library had existed in town, the successor to the Reverend William Emerson's Social Library. In 1856 the town voted to take over this organization and operate it as a public library for the benefit of the entire town, not just a limited group of subscribers. An appropriation of $100 was voted and a library committee appointed. Within a few months the committee had formulated a set of bylaws that were quickly adopted, and not long afterwards the first annual report of the library committee was presented.

The method of funding the public library is worthy of note. In most of the first few years of the library's existence as a public facility, $100 was appropriated annually at town meeting for the purpose of purchasing more books; after a decade or so the appropriation was increased to $165. This sum was to be met using the money raised by the sale of dog licenses, with any deficiency to be made up from the town's general funds.

The Civil War broke upon the nation in 1861, and Harvard was called upon to do its part. The actions of the town and its inhabitants in this war were much the same as those at the time of the Revolution and in the War of 1812 (the Mexican War did not impinge upon Harvard affairs, at least not officially). A town meeting was called on April 29, 1861 to take measures in support of the federal government.

As in past wars, resolutions were drafted and accepted. These resolutions declared the town's support of President Lincoln and his principles, and "frown[ed] indignantly upon" those who would sympathize with the South. The town then voted to pay bounties to soldiers who volunteered for active duty, in addition to any bounties which might be provided by the state or national governments. Money was then appropriated to pay these bounties.

In 1862, 1863, and 1864 quotas were levied upon Harvard, as upon all other cities and towns in the North, under which Harvard was to supply a certain number of soldiers to the Union army. As in the Revolutionary War committees were chosen to procure men to fill these quotas, and further bounties were voted to entice volunteers to fill the town's quota. There seems to have been less difficulty in meeting the quotas in the 1860s than in the 1780s. Perhaps this is because in the later years of the Revolution, the selectmen had been forced to divide the town into "classes," each "class" being responsible for hiring one soldier to be credited to Harvard; this system had worked poorly, generating disputes that lasted for years. In contrast, at a special town meeting in 1864, the town voted a $125 bounty per man to meet the last quota of the war; an informal meeting was then called immediately after the dissolution of the formal town meeting. This informal group organized itself into a society to provide more money for the soldiers, and to erect a memorial to the fifteen Harvard men who had died in active duty. The quotas were met without further ado, and less than a year later the town voted to repay to this group all the money that it had expended privately.

The efforts to erect a memorial to Harvard's Civil War dead, commenced in 1864, were not consummated until 1888, when the Civil War monument was dedicated at the southeast

SIMEON GREEN'S OLD PUPILS.

Three Generations of Them Dance in His Honor.

A Big Jollification in Harvard—The Young Old Dancing Master as Spry as When He Began with His First Class Half a Century Ago—The Town Hall Never Held Such a Gathering.

[SPECIAL DISPATCH TO THE BOSTON HERALD.]

HARVARD, Feb. 14, 1894. For over three hours tonight, in a pretty smilax-bound bower in the Harvard town hall, Dancing Master, Band Leader and Farmer Simeon Green shook hands with grandparents, their children and their children's children, who had been taught by him the graces and polish of the Terpsichorean art.

From all over Worcester county came hundreds of the former scholars of this generally beloved old gentleman to pay

SIMEON GREEN.

For more than fifty years Harvard's Simeon Green taught dancing and deportment to the boys and girls of some twenty surrounding towns. With his orchestra, made up in part of members of his own family, he conducted regular dances from 1844 to 1894; and when he retired Harvard threw a testimonial ball in his honor. (Courtesy Harvard Historical Society)

The Harvard Common in 1875, with inn and small store. (Courtesy Harvard Historical Society)

corner of the Common, where it still stands. Immediately after the war an annual appropriation for the celebration of Memorial Day was begun; in the first few years the appropriation was $25.

The Civil War left the town another legacy, perhaps more significant than a monument or a Memorial Day celebration: the legacy of a permanent debt. The town treasurer had been authorized to borrow in earlier times of heavy financial burden —during the Revolution, for example, or upon the occasion of building a new meetinghouse. But in each case the debt had been liquidated upon the passing of the crisis, and the authorization to put the town in debt had not been renewed.

In this tradition, the town treasurer was authorized in April 1863 to borrow money to cover the town's expenses, and the authorization was reaffirmed in the later years of the war. But the debt was not liquidated immediately after the conflict. The town's expenses did not return to prewar levels, and the treasurer had to borrow annually thereafter to maintain the town's finances.

Other changes in Harvard's financial operations came to pass in the years after the Civil War. Most significant would be the first attempt at financial planning. For decades the annual March meeting had considered only three "money items"— schools, highways, and town charges (the last including support of the poor). In 1859, for instance, the town voted $1,000 for highways, $1,400 for schools, and $2,500 for town charges— typical sums for the 1850s. At that same meeting the selectmen were directed to include each year, at the end of their annual report, an estimate of the following year's expenses. Apparently such estimates had never before been made.

Despite this, the town's financial arrangements did not change much for the next decade and a half, until in 1874 the town refused to make any appropriations at the March meeting, and the selectmen were again instructed to make estimates for the upcoming year. At the April meeting these estimates were ready, and appropriations were voted, this time with more detail than in the past. The first appropriation bill in the new style is here reproduced:

Schools $2,400
Highways 1,500
Interest 1,500
Repairs to schoolhouses   600
Breaking roads 600
Misc. 2,400
Poor 1,000

$10,000

We see here the substantial size of the town's debt reflected in the large amount appropriated for debt service. The budget continued at the level of about $10,000 for some years thereafter.

The system of collecting highway taxes and doing highway work also underwent a transformation during these postwar years. Up until this time, all highway work had been shared evenly by the town's populace. An appropriation was made for highway and bridge repairs, and a levy was made on each taxpayer for his share of the burden. The tax was paid not in goods or cash, but in labor—each taxpayer contributing a day or more of his own time, and perhaps also the efforts of his best pair of oxen.

From time to time proposals had been made to change the

Harvard's early road scraper. (Courtesy Harvard Historical Society)

highway tax to a money tax, but these proposals were always defeated; or, if accepted, quickly reconsidered. In the 1850s the frequency of these proposals increased, and on more than one occasion the change was made, only to be unmade at a subsequent town meeting. The proposals and counter-proposals were so frequent, and the records so vague, that it is not possible to say if a clear-cut decision was ever made on the issue. What can be said is that by the 1870s an optional system of paying highway taxes was in effect. Some people continued the old practice of contributing a small portion of their own working time to the repair of highways; we know this because the town continued to set the rates of remuneration for highway work done by individuals. Others must have opted for payment in cash, for in 1874 the surveyors of highways were instructed by the town "to hire the best help possible." Harvard did not yet have a "highway department," but large steps had been taken in this direction by eliminating the element of individual labor as a means of meeting one's highway taxes.

In 1873 Harvard moved closer to establishing a full-fledged highway department; other towns had been using "road scrapers" in their work, and a committee was chosen to see whether Harvard should obtain one of these modern conveniences. The committee reported favorably and soon the scraper was purchased. This meant of course that a building had to be provided to house the scraper, and the emerging highway department had its first physical manifestation.

The school system, too, was in a state of flux in the post–Civil War years. In 1852 a suggestion has been made that the town purchase the schoolhouses from the nine districts. This suggestion was not then accepted; but in 1864 the same proposal was made, and the schoolhouses were bought. The school districts, as corporate entities, were left intact, however; each district committee still had control over the hiring and firing of teachers, and over the details of expenditures within the districts.

But the district system as a whole was under fire, for a number of reasons. Many other towns and cities had already abandoned the district system, and a movement was underway to pass a state law abolishing school districts. In addition to the pressure felt from that effort, and perhaps more important to the townspeople of Harvard, were the problems arising from the inherent deficiencies in the system itself. The school committeemen in many districts were not the most competent available, and money was being expended carelessly and unwisely.

As a result of all these factors, the idea of abolishing the district system was presented again and again at town meetings in the 1860s. In 1869 the anti-district faction obtained a temporary victory, the town voting to eliminate the school districts. The various district school committeemen were instructed to hand over to the town clerk their financial and administrative records to be used by the new centralized committee. This new arrangement lasted only one year, however; in 1870 the town reverted to the district system.

The group opposed to districts resumed its fight, and though its proposals were unsuccessful in 1872 and 1875, in 1877 the district system was finally defeated for good. A superintendent of schools was appointed, and the district committees were relieved of their responsibility for hiring teachers. At the March meeting in 1878, the district system was officially declared dead, only four years before the commonwealth passed a law abolishing all school district systems in Massachusetts. The first recorded act of the new centralized school committee was the institution of truancy bylaws.

Simultaneous with the attempts to bring an end to the districts, but apparently of independent origins, was a move underway in Harvard to establish a high school. The district schools, of the "one-room schoolhouse" variety, did not prepare students at a sufficiently advanced level to obtain for them admission to any of the colleges in New England. Anyone aspiring to a college education had to enroll in one of the academies in Groton or Lancaster; many went to the Lawrence Academy at Groton.

The first serious attempt at establishing a high school resulted from a bequest of Mrs. Mary Whitney. In her will of 1856 she offered to donate $1,000 to the town for the purpose of

The interior of the district schoolhouse in the center of town. (Courtesy Harvard Historical Society)

This picture shows one of the last classes taught under the old district school system in Harvard; it was taken at the East Bare Hill District Schoolhouse in 1889. Front row: John Shelly, Willis Kenrick, John Callan, Fannie Kerley, Alice A. Fairbank, Alice Clark, Clara LaPage. Middle row: John Keegan, Frank Murray, Harry Chipman, Mary Keegan, Bertha Gorham, Velma Kenrick, Nettie Bemis, Annie Murray. Back row: Harry Murray, Ethel Fairbank, Sadie G. Kenrick, teacher Nella E. Welch, and Nellie, Mary, and Emma Callan. [Courtesy Harvard Historical Society]

The earliest photograph of the Bromfield School, taken by one of the teachers the year it opened. (Courtesy Harvard Historical Society)

building a high school, provided enough additional money could be raised to start such a school within ten years. The town took cognizance of this gift in 1858, but did nothing with it. In 1860 a committee was chosen to study the use of the $1,000 bequest; two years later the group reported succinctly that it would be inexpedient at that time to build such a school. A minority report by the single dissenter on the committee acknowledged the difficulty of undertaking such a project in wartime, but discussed at length the need of the town for such a school, and the desirability of making some use of the money left by Mrs. Whitney.

In 1866 a second committee was chosen to study once more the Whitney bequest. By now the Civil War was over, but it was too late; the ten-year period prescribed in Mrs. Whitney's will was over, and the money had already reverted to her heirs, or soon would.

Only a year later another, even more generous offer was made to the town by Margaret Bromfield (Pearson) Blanchard, granddaughter of Henry Bromfield. She proposed to give $4,000 to the town for a high school to be built on the old Bromfield lot, formerly the houselot of the Reverend John Seccomb. Predictably, a committee was appointed to study the proposal; and the committee reported that such a project would again not be expedient, as the town would have to make a significant financial contribution, which it was not prepared to do at that time.

Another decade passed, and on November 29, 1876 Mrs. Blanchard died. In her will she included a lengthy and detailed item, donating $20,000 and the Bromfield lot—not to the town, but to a group of trustees, who were to use the money to build the "Bromfield School." Construction was started in mid-1877, and the building was dedicated on September 12, 1878. The school, which was designed to accommodate up to one hundred students, attracted forty for the opening of classes on September 17, 1878.

Many of Harvard's public buildings were becoming quite antiquated by the time of the Civil War. The town hall had been built in 1828, and the poor farm and most of the district schoolhouses were older than that. In the post–Civil War years the town was faced with a number of construction projects to replace these old structures.

With increasing frequency in the late 1860s and the 1870s, reports were made that one or another of the schoolhouses needed to be replaced. An appropriation for repairs to the schoolhouses became an annual budget item in the later years of the 1870s, and the following extracts from the town records indicate the sad state of repair of the district No. 7 building:

> Article 6. To see if the town will remunerate Washington Warner for the loss of a cow on account of eating paint from Schoolhouse No. 7.
> [From the warrant for the November 2, 1869 meeting]

> Article 6. Voted the Selectmen be instructed to pay Mr. Warner the sum that his cow was taxed for last May.
> [From the minutes of the same meeting]

In 1863 the Shabikin schoolhouse (District No. 9) was declared inadequate and replaced. This was followed by new houses in District No. 2 in 1866 and in District No. 4 (Old Mill) in 1873. Then in 1879 the District No. 5 schoolhouse was replaced, and in 1880 two more schools were built anew—Districts No. 7 and No. 3. Clearly the financial burden of repairing and rebuilding nine different school structures was one of the factors motivating those who favored a completely centralized school system.

The poor farm had not been new when it was purchased by the town in the 1820s, and by 1868 it was declared to be hopelessly dilapidated and unworthy of repair. The erection of a new almshouse was quickly approved and money appropriated for the purpose. Construction was impeded briefly by a dispute over the precise location of the new building, but this argument was soon decided in favor of a spot near, but not exactly on, the site of the old building.

Minor arguments accompanied every such construction project in the town's history, but nothing that had gone before could compare with the extended haggling over the location and construction of a new town hall in 1870 and 1871. Warrant articles at town meetings in 1857 and 1867 called for the erection of a new town hall, but the time was not yet right, and the articles were dismissed with no action at all. In 1868 a most curious suggestion surfaced. This was only a short time after Mrs. Margaret Bromfield Blanchard had made her first offer to the town. Someone saw a chance to get two buildings for the price of one, and proposed that the Bromfield promoters and the town join forces to build a combination town hall–high school. The impracticality of this scheme, given the semiprivate nature of the Bromfield project, was quickly recognized, and the proposal was dropped.

The real fireworks began at the March meeting in 1870, when the town spent nearly a whole day voting on the question of whether or not to build a new town hall. Parliamentarians must have worn out their rulebooks that day, for the opponents of a new town hall tried every tactic available to prevent a vote in favor of such a building. They tried to claim that there were many voters absent, that the meeting should be adjourned, that the article should be postponed, and on and on. But at last the proponents of the new building carried the day, by a very narrow margin, and a committee was chosen to recommend a location and draw up plans. The following day, when the meeting was reconvened, $8,000 was appropriated for the project—nearly half the town's budget for 1870.

A month later the construction committee presented its report, which contained three principal points. First, the new town hall would cost $9,500 above the foundation—over the budget before they even began. Second, several other recently erected town halls had been examined, and the committee felt that the Harvard building should be modeled after the new Acton town hall. Finally, the site for the new building should be west of the old town hall and north of the Unitarian Church, approximately on the site formerly occupied by the Universalist meetinghouse—this is almost exactly the location of the present town hall.

This recommendation for the location of the new building set off two months of uninterrupted squabbling. The town hall committee was requested to reconsider this portion of its report. It came back two weeks later (April 18) with a lengthy discussion on the subject, noting that the committee and an engineer had

The poor farm building at it appears today. (Photo by Michael Carroll)

investigated four sites, none of which was acceptable, and asking that its original proposal be allowed to stand. The town did not agree with this, and asked the committee to try again.

On May 7 the committee reported that the town hall could be built on the site of Schoolhouse No. 1—a site bounded by the burying yard, the general store, the Congregational Church and the Common. This would require moving the schoolhouse, and either moving half a dozen graves or encroaching on the Common, to accommodate so large a building as a town hall. A week later the town voted not to move the schoolhouse and the question of the town hall's location was sent back to committee. Two more weeks passed, and the group suggested that the whole subject be postponed until the November meeting.

Six months of inactivity followed; when the town gathered on November 8, 1870 for the election of state officers and legislative representatives, no action was taken on the town hall question. The whole matter was again raised at the annual meeting the following March, but was treated as though the previous year's arguments had never occurred. An apparently routine series of votes was taken, which determined that the town would build a new town hall, and would appoint a committee to study the project. A month later, on April 3, 1871, this committee reported that the new structure should be modeled after the town hall in Westford, and should be located on the site of the then-existing town hall (across the road from the present town hall). This report was accepted, $10,000 was appropriated for the purpose, and the old town hall was sold to George L. Sawyer for $110.

Three weeks later, without explanation, the town decided to change the location of the new building, ordering that it be erected on a site just south of where the old Universalist meetinghouse had stood. This is the exact spot originally suggested more than a year earlier by the first committee, and is the site where the town hall now stands. The selectmen were ordered to obtain a lease from George L. Sawyer on the old town hall so that the town might have a place to meet, and construction of the new building was begun.

The lease arrangement lasted for a few months only, as Mr.

Sawyer wished to use the old building for purposes of his own. The October 7, 1871 town meeting and several thereafter were held in Schoolhouse No. 1. Construction proceeded quickly and the first meeting in the new town hall was held on April 1, 1872, about two years after the first decision to build.

§ The Underground Railroad

In 1850, the most stringent of a series of Fugitive Slave Acts was passed by the United States Congress; the crime of aiding a slave's escape to Canada became punishable by a fine of up to $1,000, up to six months of imprisonment, and payment of $1,000 in damages to the owner of the runaway slave. The stiff penalties were designed to dissuade northern abolitionists from participation in an illegal movement called the Underground Railroad—a secret conspiracy by which runaway slaves were transported from hideaway to hideaway, in definite steps along established routes, until they reached the freedom of Canada. Not only did federal law impose strict penalties on the "agents" and "forwarding merchants" of the Underground Railroad; federal agents actively sought to uncover the secret identities of the conspirators, even going so far as to kidnap them on occasion. But although there was an atmosphere of espionage and high adventure to the conspiracy, the federal agents did not succeed in completely shutting down the Underground Railroad. The Federal Census of 1850 indicates that approximately one thousand slaves escaped to the North that year.

Many of the escaping slaves stowed themselves away in the cargo holds of ships bringing cotton to Boston; the friendly Northern crews were usually eager to send them on their way west to Leominster and Fitchburg, two major stops on the way to Canada. Each night, a runaway would travel ten or twenty miles; in three or four nights a runaway might arrive at Harvard, where a scattering of barns and cellars offered refuge. But so fearful of discovery were the conspirators, and so sternly did they warn their children never to speak of the voices and noises they heard in their homes on the darkest nights, that the locations of many stops on the old Underground Railway remained carefully guarded secrets for years after the end of the Civil War. Doubtless some of the stops are still unknown.

Two of the more prominent agents of the "railroad" were Tower Hazard, a member of one of Harvard's oldest black families who lived on West Bare Hill, and Reuben Whitcomb, a deacon of the Harvard Congregational Church, who lived on the Common. Mary Gray Hoyt, who lived in the Whitcombs' home during the Civil War, told her daughter Mrs. Horace E. Hildreth of an occasion when Deacon Whitcomb set out for the Hazards' home late at night to beg Tower Hazard's help in comforting two terrified runaways. "I have two fugitives at my house who are so frightened and homesick for their own people that you must come and encourage them," Whitcomb is said to have pleaded. "You must give them the courage and faith to go on with their journey, for I must take them on tonight." As a black man, Hazard was a natural conspirator; but his race also placed him in great danger. A relative of his, Gardner Hazard of Leominster, had been kidnapped by federal agents who claimed he was a runaway, taken south, and sold into bondage. It was only by virtue of his literacy that he managed to convince Southern authorities that he was a free man. Nonetheless, Tower Hazard was undaunted, and contributed to the wellbeing of many fugitives in Harvard.

Much of the illegality surrounding the abolitionists' activities was justified by claiming religious principles higher than federal laws, and churchmen were frequently active in the Underground Railroad. In Harvard, the Reverend John Dodge, pastor of the Congregational church from 1854 to 1866, was a leader in the conspiracy. His granddaughter, Estelle E. Hersey, recalled in the 1930s: "My father was a boy in his early teens at the time. He says that mysterious happenings always occurred on stormy evenings or nights. They took place something like this. A wagon load of something would arrive, and his father would unload part of it in the barn. Nothing would be asked, nor would he explain anything when he returned to the house. When mealtimes arrived my father was given a bag or basket of food and was told to climb the ladder in the barn and creep along the hay to the eaves. Sometimes he dropped it in a hole, sometimes a hand shot out and took what he brought. You can imagine the thrill that came to a young boy! . . . My father was a silent partner, but he knew serious things were going on, for the air was electrified with thoughts of anti-slavery."

Mary E. Crocker, who was a helper at the Leominster station, said that stations were arranged at very short intervals all the way from Boston to Fitchburg. There were at least two intermediate stops, for instance, between Harvard and Leominster; that such short steps were common attests to the fear of discovery by federal agents. Captain Thaddeus Pollard's mansion in Still River was admirably suited for harboring refugees, since its largest room was fitted with movable partitions which provided fine hiding places. Farther from Harvard was the colonial house known as the White homestead, in North Leominster. When the White family left the area after the Civil War, they did not disclose the secret of their old house—but twenty years later the cellar floor collapsed, exposing a second cellar and a long tunnel leading to a bushy ravine near the banks of the Nashua River.

Among other known homes in and around Harvard providing refuge to runaways were the households of Simon Stone, Arad Sawyer, Captain Reuben Brown, Keep Barnard, and Avery Jones. But it is not unlikely that many other townspeople served on the Underground Railroad, as agents or as members of vigilante committees watching for "doughfaces" and "copperheads," the popular Yankee terms for anti-abolitionists. If their identities remain forever unknown, it is a tribute to their care in preserving secrecy in their efforts.

—*Jack Cushman*

§ A Soldier's Letters

These letters from the files of the Harvard Historical Society were two of several written during the Civil War from C. E. Sprague to his sister Sarah in Harvard. Badly spelled and barely punctuated, they nonetheless provide a vivid picture of the life of a Union soldier at the front.

Suffolk Va. Feb 6th 1863
Dear Sister
    . . . I suppose you have seen an account of the fight we had in the

paper but i will give you a discription of it to let you know what it is to be in such a place as we were To begin at the begining we were called out about elevn oclock p.m. and ordered into line with three days rations we started about twelve with four or five other regts and two batteries of artilery it was awful marching the mud was about four inches deep half the way. There was one place where the road run through a swamp that the water run across the road it was four inches deep in places deeper for more than a mile it was quite a novel sight to see us marching through it but not for one to experience it. When we got out about eight miles we fell in with the rebel pickets and drove them in Soon the Artilery began to fire and we were ordered up to support it just as we got there the enemy's shot and shell came flying through the woods their Battery was planted about ¾ of a mile from us. We were ordered to lay down in the woods in the rear of the guns soon the enemy's shell began to take effect. The first one killed near me was Lieut. Sawtell of Co. B Groton he was about five feet from me the same shot broke another man's leg in the same Co. Three horses and one man were killed by one shot about ten feet from me. The shot struck so near me sometimes that it filled my face with dirt that is about as near as i like to have them come the colonel and ajutant both had their horses killed. The Indiana boys a regt that have been in some of the hardest battles fought say they never saw men in a worse position than we were I thought so myself. The fact of it was the enemy had just the range of our positions and it was strange there was not more killed than there was After firing about two hours we drove them from their position followed them up shelling them in all the favorable positions drove them across the river and then started for camp where we arrived pretty well tired out. The loss in our regt was four killed and twelve wounded the whole loss on our side was about fifty killed and wounded the rebels lost more than double what we did they lost so many they could not carry them all off as our cavalry found about thirty dead round in the woods the next day. . . .   E.S.

*   *   *

Suffolk Va. March 21 1863
Dear Sister
       . . . I see by the papers that the President is about to issue a proclamation for five hundred thousand more men. I think there will be some skedadling when the draft is about to be made. I hear that there is quite a number left Littleton for the British Provinces it is thought to escape the draft. . . .   C. E. Sprague

9

THE TURN OF THE CENTURY

A new era in Harvard's affairs opened in 1881 when the annual town meeting warrant included an item asking whether women should be allowed to hold town office. The article was summarily dismissed at the time, but a survey of officeholders in that year and a few years before and after shows that a few women did hold town office even while this idea was being proposed and ignored. Mrs. George Harrod was a member of the library committee in 1879, and in 1881 Mrs. Mary Farrell was elected to a two-year term on the school committee. (This is one of the first instances of election to office for more than one year, and was part of the conversion to staggered terms for selectmen and members of some committees.) Apparently the question brought before the town meeting referred only to the principal town offices—selectman, treasurer, clerk, moderator, assessor—and did not include minor town offices.

Whatever the intention was, the influence of women in town affairs continued to increase in the teeth of male opposition during the closing years of the nineteenth century. The 1881 proposal for granting women the right to hold office was revived in 1883, with the added request that they also be allowed to vote in town affairs. Although the request could not be summarily dismissed the second time around, the vote when taken was heavily against the desires of the women. At the November meeting in 1895, after the votes for state and county officers, the town voted on the question of whether or not women should be allowed "municipal suffrage," a question that was being considered statewide. In this instance the votes were recorded: 39 for, 82 against, and 42 blanks. As a paradoxical addendum, there is recorded also the vote of Harvard's women—19 for, 0 against—on the question of whether women should vote in town affairs.

Even in the face of these defeats, women continued to serve on the library and school committees, and, as will be shown, a

ANTI-SUFFRAGE

MEETING

AT THE

Town Hall, Harvard

FRIDAY, AUGUST 20

At 8.00 P. M.

Not all Harvard women were in favor of suffrage for their sex. (Courtesy Harvard Historical Society)

group of 140 women had great influence in settling a long dispute over the location of the town's new cemetery. The movement for women's political rights had not yet reached full bloom, but the seeds had been sown.

Other changes in the holding of town offices were occurring in the 1880s and 1890s. For decades Harvard had managed to collect its taxes without having the permanent office of tax collector. In the earliest years of the town's history, taxes had been collected by the elected constables, but this had not been satisfactory. For most of the nineteenth century, the position of tax collector had been let out by auction, with the lowest bidder also routinely being chosen constable. This began to change in 1885, when the collector was chosen from among the lowest bidders; the lowest bidder was no longer assured of getting the post. The position underwent further evolution in 1892 when a fixed salary was set (usually about $90 or $100), and from 1893 onward the tax collector was an elected, salaried town officer, and was no longer chosen constable.

The constable, shorn of all tax-collecting duties, now had the task of circulating town meeting warrants, in addition to acting as an officer of the peace. In 1883 the selectmen appointed for the first time a "special police," no doubt to maintain order on the Fourth of July or election day. In later years two special police might be appointed, but there was still no full-time police department.

At various times in the nineteenth century, Harvard's inhabitants had voted to purchase odds and ends of fire equipment—engines (i.e., hand-tubs), extinguishers, ladders, buckets. This equipment had been housed at various places around the Common, sometimes in the same building with the town hearse or the road-scraper. At a town meeting on June 2, 1892, $1,200 was appropriated to buy "two 55 gallon Holloway Hand Machines," apparently the latest word in fire-fighting technology. One of these was housed at the center and one at Still River, and a month later an informal list of "engine men" was inserted in the town records—five men in "Harvard No. 1" and five men in "Still River No. 2."

For a brief period in the 1890s the town abandoned the old method of dealing with highways, which involved dividing the town into districts, each of which was maintained by a surveyor and a crew of men working under him. In 1890, under pressure no doubt from the state, Harvard abolished the districts and instead of surveyors elected three road commissioners who had jurisdiction over the entire town. This system lasted only until 1894 when the town reverted to the district system. These changes are reminiscent of the early steps in the centralization of the school system, where the districts were briefly abandoned for a partial centralization, followed after only one year by a return to the district system, but eventually being completely centralized. The highway maintenance system, too, would later be permanently centralized, but not for many years. An attempt in 1901 to discontinue the highway districts and appoint road commissioners, as in the years from 1890 to 1894, was voted down; and no more is heard about the matter for many years.

All of these changes—increased institutionalization of tax collection, and the movement toward more permanent fire, police, and highway departments—were but chapters in the long story of the decrease in town reliance on voluntarism and the increase in differentiated institutions and minor bureaucracies.

The 1860s and 1870s had seen the beginnings of large-scale philanthropy in Harvard. The Mary Whitney bequest of $1,000 for a high school was followed by the even more magnanimous gift from Henry Bromfield's granddaughter, which resulted in the establishment of the Bromfield School in 1879. This philanthropic movement expanded in the 1880s and 1890s, both in the number and the magnitude of the bequests.

An unusually large number of legacies were offered to Harvard's townspeople in 1886. At the town meeting held on April 5 of that year, the wishes of Edward Lawrence were made known to the town. Lawrence, a former resident of Harvard, but living in Charlestown at the time of his death, provided funds for the construction of a new stone wall around the center cemetery. More significant was Lawrence's gift of $5,000 to be used for the purchase of new books for the public library. The

Scene on the Harvard Common shortly after the building of the library.
(Courtesy Harvard Historical Society)

magnitude of this offer can be judged when we remember that the town had never appropriated more than $200 in any one year for the same purpose; Lawrence's bequest was greater than the total amount appropriated for the library since the town had taken over that institution more than thirty years before. The gift was conditional, however; Lawrence would allow the money to be given to the town only if Harvard provided a new and secure building to house the volumes purchased from his funds.

Fortunately another gift was offered at the same town meeting which made it possible for the town to comply with that stipulation. The trustees of the estate of Hannah W. C. Sawyer announced that Mrs. Sawyer in her will had earmarked the greater part of her estate, which came to more than $5,000, to be used for the construction and maintenance of a library building in Harvard. Mrs. Sawyer's trustees had already acted without consulting the town as a whole, purchasing for $450 the Old Hotel lot as the most suitable site for the erection of the new library building. The Old Hotel lot was the former site of the

Wetherbee Tavern; this location had become available in 1880 when the tavern and the adjacent dwelling of Asa Daby were totally destroyed in a fire of suspicious origin.

The town responded by appointing a committee to meet with the Sawyer trustees. This committee returned very quickly with plans for a building which would cost $6,500; the Sawyer estate would supply $3,500 of this amount (as well as the lot already purchased), and the town would make up the difference. The plans included a room in the southwest corner of the building to be used as the town's post office. When the motion on this item was put to a vote, 71 were in favor and 61 against, and for the first time in Harvard's history a complete list of those voting, and their positions on the vote, was included in the town records!

The town appropriated $3,500, the tax assessment to be spread out over a number of years; Harvard architect William Channing Whitney donated his services; and construction was begun almost immediately. Before it had proceeded very far, yet another gift was received by the town; on July 21, 1886 Warren Hapgood offered $2,500 to finance a number of improvements on the original plans, and later increased this amount by $100. Construction proceeded rapidly and at the annual meeting in March 1887 the library building committee reported that nearly $10,000 had been expended, this amount being about equally divided among the town, Warren Hapgood, and the estate of Mrs. Sawyer. Tablets commemorating Harvard's Civil War participants were installed at the library's entrance, and the building was dedicated on June 22, 1887. In 1902 Warren Hapgood made another bequest for a substantial addition on the east side of the library; this was the last enlargement of the building, aside from the space gained upon the relocation of the post office.

This tangible monument to culture in Harvard apparently served as a stimulus to other philanthropists, for in 1890 Henry L. Warner (a former Harvard resident who had removed to Des Moines, Iowa) made arrangements to give the town $10,000 for the establishment of a series of public lectures. These lectures were to be patterned on the Lowell Lectures in Boston, and were to be educational in nature; such controversial matters as religion and partisan politics were to be avoided, but there were no other restrictions on the subjects that might be expounded. The town officially accepted the gift on March 2, 1891, and a board of trustees was appointed, the first and foremost being E. A. Hildreth. Thus were established the Warner Free Lectures, which have continued uninterrupted for more than eight decades.

Soon after establishing these lectures, Henry L. Warner became involved in another project of public improvement—the establishment of a new cemetery—but not until the project was nearly completed. As the years passed the old burying yard at the center had become more and more crowded, and from time to time in the 1880s suggestions were made at town meeting that a new cemetery be established, or that additions be made to the old one. Nothing positive was done until March 4, 1889, when the cemetery committee was instructed to consider sites for a new graveyard. On April 22 the committee reported that it would be impractical to expand the cemetery at the center, since it was hemmed in on three sides by the Common, the highway, and the Bromfield School, while the fourth side was either too swampy or too rocky. A number of alternative locations were suggested, including one near the intersection of Slough Road and Bolton Road, and one on Depot Road opposite Mill Road. The committee recommended the latter.

Apparently the recommendation did not meet with approval from most of the citizens of Harvard, for no action was taken in 1889, and on April 7, 1890, the cemetery committee was instructed to purchase additional land next to the old cemetery. After a short adjournment the committee reported that it might be possible to obtain some meadowland from Mr. H. F. Whitney; perhaps as much as a third of this land was useless because of sunken boulders, but still it would be a substantial addition. Another year passed, and on March 2, 1891 the committee told the assembled townspeople that Mr. Whitney wanted $2,000 for four acres—an exorbitant price, the committee felt, for land of such poor quality. This must have convinced the majority of interested citizens that an addition to the center

Henry Harrod's blacksmith shop. (Courtesy Harvard Historical Society)

cemetery was impossible, for the cemetery committee immediately went to work searching out suitable new sites.

On May 27, 1891 the committee was ready with a new report; it presented suggestions on seven sites scattered around town, including the Dickinson lot on Depot Road opposite Mill Road (previously proposed), and a new lot owned by A. H. Turner, on a small hill about halfway between the center and Still River. After presenting this list to the townspeople, a vote was taken; more than half the voters chose the Dickinson lot, and not a single ballot opted for the Turner lot. Twelve hundred dollars was appropriated for the cemetery committee and work was begun immediately.

At the following year's annual March meeting, Henry L. Warner, the donor of money for free lectures, made his first contribution to the new cemetery, offering to provide for the new graveyard an arched stone entranceway. This was accepted, and in April the site was officially designated Brookside Cemetery. Terms were set for the purchase of individual and family lots, and the first body was soon interred. At last Harvard had its new cemetery—or so it seemed.

On September 17, 1892 a special town meeting was called to consider yet another proposal from Mr. Warner. This time Warner wanted to reopen debate on the location of the new burying yard, even though the Brookside site was already in use. He felt that Brookside was not sufficiently dignified and scenic for a cemetery, pointing out that other near neighbors of Harvard had created new cemeteries on hillsides with splended views, rather than in low-lying flatlands, hemmed in by brooks and swamps. The townspeople voted down this proposal, but did appoint a committee to meet with Mr. Warner to consider his objections at greater length.

A week later this committee reported on its discussion with Mr. Warner, who had reiterated his dissatisfaction with the Brookside location, and berated Harvard's citizens for their lack of interest in a project which should have been a symbol of civic pride. In pursuing his objective, Warner also managed to strike a blow for women's suffrage, arguing that the new cemetery site had been chosen by male voters only, and that if women's opinions were to be taken into account, his proposal would be accepted. In support of this Mrs. E. Farwell and 139 other Harvard women presented a petition siding with Warner.

This first major political action by Harvard's women was probably a determining factor in the committee's decision to urge compliance with Warner's proposal, which in the meantime had become more specific. Warner suggested that the cemetery be moved to a site on a hill owned by A. H. Turner and Henry R. Harrod, on the road from the center to Still River. This was almost exactly the same site proposed in May 1891, which had not received a single vote at that time. Warner also offered to donate an additional $1,000 if this land was accepted.

At the March meeting in 1893 Warner's proposal was officially adopted. There were a number of minor problems involved in this move. One body had already been buried at Brookside; the family readily gave permission for its transferral to the new location. The stone portal donated by Warner had already been delivered to Brookside, and was partially erected; arrangements were made with the contractor to move the stone to the new site once the weather improved. Fencing had to be provided on three sides of the lot; money was quickly appropriated to that end. Mr. Warner was allowed to suggest a name for the new cemetery. He chose Bellevue, an obvious reference to one of his principal arguing points in his proposal for relocation. Finally, in the spring of 1893, Harvard did have a new cemetery.

What became of Brookside? The town owned the land, but it could no longer be used for its original purpose. For some years the sole use was as a gravel pit for highway work. In 1910 the town tried to sell the land, as it had more gravel pits than needed; but the sale was not made. The old Brookside site has continued to be used for many purposes by the highway department and has, of course, acquired yet another use—that of the town dump, later the sanitary landfill.

These acts of philanthropy and others that had gone before had in most cases ended with the philanthropist's name being attached to the product of his or her philanthropy—the Bromfield School, the Hapgood wing of the library, the Warner Free Lecture Fund. But perhaps the most philanthropic citizens of Harvard have not been so memorialized; the various members of the Hildreth family—in particular the brothers Edwin A. and Stanley B.—contributed greatly to the cultural and esthetic improvement of the town, without having their name perpetuated in the same fashion as Bromfield, Hapgood, and Warner. This family was active in many ways. Edwin was a trustee of the estate of Mrs. Sawyer, which contributed so much to the erection of the library building; he was also a trustee of the Warner Free Lecture Fund. Stanley invested much time and energy in efforts to beautify the Common and improve the town's water system. But perhaps the greatest contribution of the Hildreth family was the support they provided for the construction projects involved in the centralization of the town's school system.

The long-established district school system had for years been under attack. The town had taken over control of the system in 1878, but classes were still held in the districts after that date. The small one-room schoolhouses were becoming outmoded at an increasing rate, and the expenditures for repair or replacement of these school buildings were mounting rapidly.

At left is the early general store run by Gale and Dickson before they converted it to a grain annex. At right is the center district schoolhouse. (Courtesy Harvard Historical Society)

Gale and Dickson's general store after it moved into the new flat-roofed building. (Courtesy Mrs. Wallace Bryant)

The first district school to be abandoned was that in Shabikin, District No. 9. On April 3, 1882 the town appropriated $130 for transporting the District No. 9 students to the center district schoolhouse—the first instance of busing in Harvard. In 1896 the building of the north Still River district was also abandoned, and the appropriation for "conveying scholars from one district to another" became an annual item of town business. By the turn of the century this amounted to as much as $1,000 yearly.

A proposal for the erection of a single school at the center was put before the town at the annual meeting in 1903, but was indefinitely postponed. The matter was urgent, however, and the following year, with the encouragement of the Hildreth family, the subject was again included in the warrant for the April meeting of 1904. The Hildreths had already investigated the availability of land, and had found that two parcels of land from the Savage estate were on the market. These two pieces of land were next to one another, across the road from the Bromfield School; both were suitable locations for a new school. The Hildreths proposed to give this land to the town and throw in an additional $3,000, if the town would shoulder the remainder of the financial burden. The town did not hesitate to appropriate $9,000, and the new school building was quickly erected.

The new center school (which over the years came to be known as the Brown Building because of its color) was dedicated on June 2, 1905. The selectmen were authorized to sell the old District No. 1 schoolhouse, and eventually all the abandoned district schoolhouses were sold. The District No. 1 schoolhouse was removed from its location just north of the old burying yard, between the general store and the Congregational Church; and the park commissioners were authorized to spend $100 beautifying and landscaping the now vacant lot.

With the removal of the District No. 1 schoolhouse in 1905, the Harvard Common took on much the same appearance that it shows today. All the public buildings—library and town hall— and churches were in place; the Civil War monument and a memorial flagstaff had been erected. The state highway (Route 111) had been built through the center in 1895; now unnecessary roads were eliminated, and those roads that were retained were provided with curbing, drains, and in some cases pavement. Perhaps the only significant change in the next six decades was the addition in 1912 of overhead electrical and telephone wires, and the accompanying poles.

The business community in Harvard, too, was flourishing at the turn of the century. The general store, built in 1851 to replace an earlier store that had been destroyed by fire, provided the community with everything from plows to pianos under the ownership of Henry Gale and Philip O. Dickson. In 1896 the level-topped general store building was built, and the old structure became the grain annex that supplied the farmers with feed. Albert Bigelow's butcher shop operated from its small building on Old Littleton Road just behind the present "Inn." William Hanna, a man with a reputation for vigor and fun, had bought the stage route through Harvard in 1892; he delivered mail, packages, and people from depots to dwellings until 1912. Fiske Warren had driven the first car in Harvard—the first, he claimed, in the state of Massachusetts—as early as 1896, but the horse and carriage still dominated the streets, served by Hildreth's Horse Powered Machines, one of Harvard's few large industries, and by the Harrods' blacksmith shops operating in Still River and on Littleton Road.

Still River took advantage of its proximity to the railroad station, and business thrived there as well. The New England Brick Company and the Union Paving Company were both located near the tracks, and Haskell's Vinegar Works supplied its wares to buyers all over the state. By the 1920s, Still River would be one of the largest dairying areas in Massachusetts, boasting of putting more milk on the train line than any other town. In fact, dairying was the major occupation in Harvard during the early years of the twentieth century.

During this same period at the end of the nineteenth century, a burst of creative energy evidenced itself in the remarkable number of patented inventions that emerged from Harvard workshops. Between 1851 and 1930, 141 separate patents—including ones for the broom corn sorter, the circular saw, the steam-powered wood splitter, the electric light socket, and the paper cup—were issued to Harvard residents. Among the more productive of these ingenious men and women were the Shakers Elijah Myrick and Tabitha Babbitt, the Hildreth brothers, George Wright, George Burt, and Norman Marshall.

The long string of philanthropic actions by Harvard's citizens was paralleled by an increased consciousness of the town's history, much of this interest promoted by the philanthropists themselves. In 1891 Warren Hapgood proposed to Henry Stedman Nourse of Lancaster the project of writing a history of Harvard. Nourse agreed immediately; drawing upon his unexcelled knowledge of the history of the Nashua River Valley, he was able to publish in 1894 his volume of town history, the financial burden being undertaken by Warren Hapgood. The decades around the turn of the century witnessed the peak of local historical activity in New England, and Nourse's history still stands as one of the best local histories of its period.

In 1897 was founded the Harvard Historical Society, which for many years was housed in the upper room of the public library building. One of the prime movers in the establishment of this society was E. A. Hildreth, who was elected its first treasurer. When Hildreth died in 1907 the town voted a testimonial resolution honoring this man and his many benefactions to the town. No public building or institution is attached to the Hildreth name, but the 1907 vote of the town recognizes the great accomplishments of the Hildreth family as a whole, and symbolizes the many philanthropic and humanistic acts that altered and improved Harvard in the decades before and after 1900.

§ Remembering the Shakers

The following reminiscences of the Harvard Shakers are excerpted from a series of newspaper articles written in the 1930s by Arthur T. West, who lived among the Shakers from 1884 to 1889 and was the teacher in their district school for several years starting in 1895. Mr. West also served the town for a time as postmaster and as a member of the school committee.

To know the Shakers one must have lived among them and to fully understand their inner lives one must have loved the Shakers. The casual visitor among Shakers never could really get to know them. . . .

Their hour of worship was from ten to eleven o'clock on Sunday morning. There was always a full attendance. Only serious physical disability prevented one's attendance. If such a thing should happen today in any one of our churches the minister would think the millenium had arrived for sure. At about ten minutes before the hour all the brothers and sisters gathered in the Bell house. Here they waited, sitting in respectful silence. At the stroke of the big bell they rose and left the house, elders and eldresses leading, and in single file, crossing the road by different walks, and entering the meetinghouse, the brothers at the left entrance and the sisters at the right entrance.

They marched to the center of the room, forming in ranks of six or seven, facing to the center. When in formation they were standing in ranks, the brothers being separated from the sisters by about six feet and facing each other. The elders and eldresses were, as would be assumed, at the head of the ranks, and so on down the lines to the boys and girls. A moment of silence and then by previous arrangement a sister starts a song. There is no musical instrument to lead, for this was not allowed in Shaker meeting. This song was always of slow movement. All joined in at once keeping time with a slight up and down movement of the forearms with palms up.

It should be said here that except while singing the hands were always clasped across the front on a level with the elbows. During singing the hands kept the up and down movement to the rhythm of the song. Following the opening song one of the elders made a few remarks. These remarks were along the line of daily conduct with no idea of sermonizing. In fact while the Shakers were strong believers in the Bible that book was never used in their hour of worship. A second song was sung and then more remarks by the head eldress.

Suddenly a change comes over the gathering. A march song is started. The ranks of the brothers and sisters break. The elders cross the room as the rest of the brothers fall in, forming a double line. The sisters start forward and almost as if by magic the assembly is marching around the room in double lines, singing their march song, keeping time with their hands and with a very slight upward spring in each step. By previous arrangement four sisters and a brother form a hollow square in the center of the room. These were selected for their vocal qualifications and they led in the singing. At the conclusion of the song all stopped and faced the center of the room with hands clasped in front. Then came words of testimony and wisdom from different sisters and brothers, interspersed with march songs and the accompanying marching as long as the song lasted.

The testimonies from these elderly sisters and brothers impress me even now as being so simple and sincere. I shall always remember a very old lady, Sister Hahaleth, always concluding her remarks with these words: "I know I love the Lord." This she would repeat with the accent on "know." The elders and eldresses gave words of wisdom in their remarks. Eldress Annie frequently said: "You know it is the little foxes that spoil the corn," and then went on to admonish those present to attend to the small things in life and the larger problems would never appear.

*   *   *

The second house, so called [across the road from the Shaker meetinghouse], was used mainly for living quarters for the sisters. In this building lived the family doctor, Sister Mary Robbins, the most wrinkled and the sweetest old lady I think I ever knew. With her knowledge of the many species of herbs and their medicinal value she kept the family in good health. No yeast, ex-lax, cod liver oil or cosmetics were necessary to keep in condition as long as Sister Mary was in charge. She would produce a drink that would restore one to normal. . . .

. . . [N]o conversation was allowed at the family table and this might prove irksome to visitors. And here let me say that Elder Elijah, often a guest at the home of Mr. and Mrs. Edwin Hildreth of this town, enjoyed the sociability at the table in the conversation always prominent at the meals at this home—yet the rule was never broken but once in all my memory, and then the offending sister was given many dark frowns from her sister members, although only three words were spoken. . . .

Sister Mary Hill, who fell at the age of seventy-two and broke her hip, was told by Dr. Cowles that she never would be able to walk again.

This was very much resented by Sister Mary and to prove her ability about a year later walked to Ayer and called on the doctor himself. However, a Shaker team was necessary to rescue the old lady and return her home.

*   *   *

About 1846 the town began the general renovation of its school buildings, all the buildings in town being remodeled, and in some instances entirely rebuilt, except the Shaker school, which alone needed neither rebuilding nor repairing. The first superintendent in 1878 speaks of it as "kept in most perfect order," and notes the fact that "after 50 years the desks were almost as good as new," due, no doubt, to the wholesome respect the Shaker pupils had for the school committee man, always one of the older Shaker elders. School books were kept in the same good order, for a torn book meant for the guilty one to pay a visit for stern reproof from the severe elder brother to whom the report was made. . . .

The Shaker school consisted of one room, heated by an old airtight stove, fed with good chunks of hard wood—and it may be said we were always warm. The Shakers furnished seats for visitors—one large Windsor chair, one Shaker ladder-back, and two rockers. No wonder that Supt. Clay in his visits to the school, seated in one of the old rockers near enough to the heater to be comfortable, found it hard to leave and often remarked to me that "this is the best school in town." . . .

. . . It was during the winter of 1896-7 some very instructive lectures were being put on by the trustees of the Warner Lecture Fund. The writer, then a teacher in the Shaker school, conceived the idea of arranging for the girls of the school to attend one of these illustrated lectures. The first step was to interview the family eldress, Annie Walker. Her attitude was favorable, but conditional upon the consent of Eldress Eliza Babbitt of the ministry elders. Here let me explain that the family eldress had charge of the family affairs as a mother over her family. The ministry elders were the authority on business matters or matters calling for a direct change in the general affairs of the village.

This idea of going out nights to attend affairs in the hall of the town was a very decided departure from Shaker custom. Eldress Eliza was firm and her answer was "nay." My girls were awaiting the verdict and their teacher was already tardy for the afternoon session. But, as Sister Catherine [Mr. West's grandmother] always said, "He that putteth his hand to the plow," etc., gave me courage and I dwelt on the educational value of these lectures. The girls would be properly chaperoned; seats at the hall would be reserved for them; Brother Frank would drive the barge, and Eldress Annie would guarantee safe return to the village. At

last Eldress Maria said "ye" and with the odds all against her Eldress
Eliza finally gave consent, and much to my amusement when the
Shaker party arrived at the hall that night who should be with the girls
but Eldress Maria herself. . . .

What a pleasant sight it was to those of us who can recall to see the
Shakers drive into town—a light express wagon drawn by a splendid
draft horse with the two sisters on the back seat and a brother driving
on the front seat. There was something so restful in their appearance. A
drive through the village or a visit—they always gave one that sense of
peacefulness and contentment. . . .

Of course there were some love affairs between the boys and girls.
Notes were passed in school and secret meetings were held, when to all
Shaker rules everyone should have been safely tucked away in bed.
These affairs were sometimes found out by the elders and those
offending were sent away from the village. Today, if one may judge
from present Shaker conditions, such a thing as a love affair would not
be considered a major offense. But I speak of the old days, when there
were real Shakers.

*   *   *

At the end of these very happy days of teaching the town decided
to consolidate all the outlying districts. The Shakers, seeing disaster to
their colony, protested the move and promised to keep the numbers in
their school above fifteen pupils if they could be permitted to retain
their school. But the committee were adamant and I think very
unreasonable. The loss of their young people from the village was
disastrous to their welfare, and from that time the old people, deprived
of the young folks, began to slip, and the result was the eventual loss of
the colony from town.

The loss of taxes more than offset the saving to the town of the
expense of the school. Financially it was a very poor move on the part
of the committee with no gain whatever in the schooling. As the young
folks now in the village reach school age it can be readily seen that
transportation alone will become quite an item. What the loss of these
thrifty and peaceful people means to the town can be readily seen by the
ruins and desolation of this once prosperous village. So passed the
Shaker school.

10
BETWEEN TWO WARS

With the coming of World War I, Harvard was again called upon to do its share; but the world and the nation had changed, and the form of the town's response was also changed. In past major conflicts Harvard's townspeople had been called upon to participate directly in obtaining recruits for military service, and in raising all or a portion of the pay of these recruits, including substantial bounties. In the twentieth century things were to be done differently. The federal government had grown stronger, and many duties formerly performed on a local level had been incorporated into the operations of the national government. Thus, a local draft board, part of a national network, removed any necessity for the town government to take an active part in supplying men for the armed forces.

Harvard men and women did go to war, of course, and the people of the town, deprived of intimate participation in the recruitment process, still wanted to show their appreciation. Miss Clara Endicott Sears organized many of the town's teenaged girls into the "Canning and Evaporating Club of Harvard," which supplied foodstuffs to nearby soldiers. The Red Cross tea room on the Common benefited the humanitarian relief effort as well. In May 1919, a special town meeting appropriated $700 to provide a welcome home to "our boys." And in 1920 the memorial flagstaff in the southwestern corner of the Common was erected to honor the World War I dead.

The most far-reaching consequence of the war to Harvard was the incorporation of a large chunk of the town's northwestern corner in Camp Devens. The United States Army saw the tract of land where Harvard, Lancaster, Shirley, and Ayer came together as a most suitable spot for a training facility, and in 1916 and 1917 began purchasing land in this area. The portion of Harvard taken included everything north of Still River Depot and west of the railroad tracks—in other words, the Plum Tree Meadows and most of the Shabikin district.

Camp Devens, later to be named Fort Devens, was used extensively during the few years of the war, but with the coming of peace, the facility was partially deactivated. The southern section of the post, including some of the Harvard portion, continued to be used for occasional National Guard training, especially artillery practice. But the Army's need for the land was not great, and a few of the residents were allowed to remain in their homes and continue to live much as they had before the military came. In 1920 Harvard voted to discontinue all town roads within the limits of Camp Devens, even though some Harvard citizens remained there.

With the coming of World War II military activities at Devens were of course expanded, and the remaining residents of the preempted land had to leave. Since that time the land has been used for military purposes only, but not until mid-1975 was the last of the old dwellings in Shabikin razed.

Part of the Devens land, corresponding to the old Plum Tree Meadows region, was for some time administered by the Army as a wildlife refuge. But in an economy move in the early 1970s the Army was directed to divest itself of its less important lands, so in 1974 the meadows were turned over to the United States Fish and Wildlife Service. The region is now operated as the Oxbow National Wildlife Refuge and may be freely visited, although it is still technically within the limits of Fort Devens and is still used for military activities to a limited extent. This land is interesting for the migratory fowl and other wildlife that

Camp Devens supply team on the Harvard Common during World War I. (Courtesy Harvard Historical Society)

can be observed, but there is also historical interest in the Plum Tree Meadows; for this is some of the first land granted in the old Lancaster part of Harvard, and one can still see the remains of the causeway that carried the Union Turnpike on its way to Leominster in the early years of the nineteenth century.

The establishment of Camp Devens meant more to the town than the loss of more than five thousand acres of land. Harvard still did not have a permanent police force, and the influx of military trainees in large numbers created problems that the part-time constables were unable to handle. The town records for September 15, 1917 note that "Special Constables [were] sworn on above date with headquarters at Ayer . . . to serve in this and other towns around Camp Devens without expense to the towns." At the end of the war the special constabulary force was discontinued, and Harvard returned to its prewar policy of depending on the constables and the occasional "special police." Not until February 1, 1932 was a permanent police force proposed, and even then no action was taken.

The police department as a permanent, organized institution had not yet come into existence; but in the years between the wars, the fire department and the highway department became full-fledged organizations. On March 16, 1914 a warrant article asked for money to repair the room in the town hall that housed the fire equipment. Nothing was done immediately, but on November 3 of the same year, the town voted to buy a number of the privately owned horse sheds just west of the town hall. The horse sheds were falling into disuse with the increased use of motor vehicles, and they were now to be converted so that they could house the town's fire and highway equipment.

In 1916 and 1917 the town purchased new fire equipment — motorized fire engines to replace the horse-drawn engines both at the center and in Still River. A forest-fire engine had been bought in 1912. Equipment for highway work was also being acquired more frequently: a steam roller in 1915, a dump truck in 1922, and several snowplows. With all this added equipment of an increasingly diversified and sophisticated nature, the converted horse sheds soon proved inadequate. By now, the town records were referring frequently to "the fire department" and "the highway department," although neither had been officially organized as such. In 1921 the town unanimously voted $6,000 for the erection of a new building to house the recently acquired fire equipment, and this building was quickly constructed on the site of some of the old horse sheds. At a town meeting on May 12, 1926 the fire department was officially given the authority and the responsibility for fighting fires in Harvard, under the direction of Bill Perry, its first chief.

The highway department, as we have seen, was also outgrowing its quarters in the horse sheds. The old Brookside cemetery site had been used for many years as a gravel pit for highway work, and on February 3, 1930, $3,000 was voted to be used for tearing down the last of the horse sheds on the Common and building sheds at Brookside to house the various pieces of highway equipment. The fire and highway departments were now full grown, independent creatures, installed in their own new houses.

While these two institutions were crystallizing, another old town institution was being dismantled. On more than one occasion proposals had been put forward for Harvard to discontinue its poor farm and make an agreement with one or more neighboring towns for the joint care of their poor. Finally, in early 1916, an ad hoc committee reported back to the town that the poor farm should be closed down and sold. No concrete plan for the care of the poor in the future was set forth, but the report noted that Groton was willing to take in the town's poor. The committee suggested a price of $9,000 for the poor farm, reserving a small tract of land for a gravel pit, and reserving also the gravesite, just off Poor Farm Road in what is now the Town Forest, of Captain Benjamin Stewart of Boston, "who died of the small pox June 16th, 1775 in ye 45 year of his age."

Thus matters stood for several years, for no one could be found who was willing to put up $9,000. On April 5, 1923 the town agreed that the price should be reduced to $7,000; if no sale were made by October 1, the poor farm would be put up for auction. In September an offer of $6,500 was made, but not accepted. At last the auction was held, and the poor farm was sold for slightly more than $7,000. The poor farm no longer existed; the few remaining paupers were transferred to state, county, and private institutions.

The public schools changed only slightly in the 1920s and 1930s. Children in the first eight grades attended school at the Brown Building in the center. Those who advanced to high school went either to Bromfield, which continued to be run as a private institution, or to a private school or a public high school in a neighboring town. During the 1920s it became obvious that the Brown Building was not sufficient for the town's needs. In 1924 the town signed a five-year agreement with the Bromfield trustees whereby the town was allowed to use a portion of the Bromfield building for the lower grades. This was not of course a permanent solution, and in 1928 a committee was appointed to consider the problem of overcrowding in the public school. This committee reported that no major building projects were necessary at that time, and for the next decade the problem of overcrowding did not attract much attention.

By the end of the 1930s overcrowding in the schools again gained prominence, and in 1939 Harvard decided upon a plan of expanding the elementary school. This construction program was carried out by 1940; in the meantime the town had assumed

Fire at the Inn on the Harvard Common, 1917. (Courtesy Mrs. Ruth Muller)

management of the Bromfield School. The Bromfield trustees had fallen into a financial bind, not having sufficient income from the trust to keep Bromfield running. The trustees and the town therefore agreed to a plan under which the town would pay the trustees one dollar a year for the use of the building; the trustees would apply part of their trust income to the maintenance of the building and turn the rest over to the town. Thus, by the end of 1940 Harvard had a full twelve-grade public school system, and, for the moment, sufficient space. But this transformation of the public school system just before World War II would seem insignificant when compared to the changes that were to come in the postwar years.

Dairying continued as the primary farm activity in Harvard up until the 1940s, though as refrigeration techniques enabled fewer men to keep more cattle the number of smaller farms declined. Also a growing industry on the hillsides of Harvard were the apple orchards, whose owners took advantage of technological advances to contribute to their large crops and burgeoning reputations. A few scattered poultry farms—one on East Bare Hill, one in Still River, one at the Old Mill—rounded out the agricultural picture.

The general store on the Common had passed into the ownership of William Kerley, Reuben Reed, and Wallace Bryant, who ran it with few changes from the Gale and Dickson days. Bigelow expanded his operations to include some groceries; another small food store was started next to the Post Office by Mr. and Mrs. Henry Dickson; and Still River had its market as well, run by Walter Viles.

Train service had been on the decline since the beginning of the century, and in 1933 the Still River and Harvard station agents were dismissed, but the Boston and Maine Railroad ran a bus between Ayer and Clinton for the convenience of Harvard rail passengers. The new state highway Route 110 had been built from Clinton through the Harvard Common, making the center of town a crossroads, but the anticipated rush of commercial activity did not ensue.

The Agassiz Station of the Harvard University Astronomical Observatory was established in 1932, following the gift of thirty acres of land at the Pinnacle on top of Oak Hill (the highest point in Harvard) from the Reverend and Mrs. Alfred C. Fuller. Optical instruments at the observatory include a 61-inch reflector telescope, a 24-inch reflector telescope, and several photographic reflectors. A 60-foot parabolic radio telescope antenna was installed in 1956, then replaced in 1967 by an 84-foot antenna. In addition to use by students and faculty of the Harvard University astronomy program, the station is used by the Astrophysical Observatory of the Smithsonian Institution in its work on the optical tracking and analysis of earth satellites.

The 1820s and 1830s had been in one sense the peak of religious activity in Harvard, for at that time there flourished a greater number of denominations than at any time before or since. The First Congregational Church had recently split into two differing churches—the Unitarian and the Evangelical Congregational, of about equal size and strength. The Baptist church had experienced great growth at the end of the eighteenth century, and the Shakers were at the height of their activity. The Methodist and the Universalist churches, although small, were very active.

A century later the religious scene had changed greatly. Three of these religious groups had disappeared completely, and one was rapidly fading away, leaving only two churches still in good health. The Universalist and Methodist churches were the shortest-lived of all, both having disbanded before the Civil War. The members of these churches were left with the choice of joining one of the other churches in town, or of traveling on the Sabbath to the nearest town which had a church of their denomination.

The disappearance of the Shakers was a different story. The faith of most of the Shakers never wavered, but as the years passed they were unable to gain new converts. Their doctrines of course did not allow replenishment of their numbers from within, so that as the nineteenth century wore on and the members grew older and died, the Shaker population began slowly to decline. This was happening in all the other Shaker communities as well, and from time to time various Shaker villages would be abandoned, the members moving to join another small community nearby. Time ran out for the Harvard Shakers in 1918, when the few remaining Believers decided to join their comrades in Canterbury, New Hampshire, where a handful of Shakers can still be found.

The Baptist church had not folded, but very few members remained, and by the 1940s the Baptists could no longer support a church in Harvard. After nearly 170 years the Baptists were forced to dissolve their church. The building was eventually sold to the Harvard Historical Society for use as its headquarters, thus freeing space that the society had previously been using in the library.

The two churches that continued to prosper were the Unitarian and the Congregational. Both had remained strong since their separation in 1821. Evidence of this strength is seen in the requests both made to the town in 1923; each church asked for a small portion of the Common adjoining the existing churches so that additions might be built. These requests were granted. The Congregational Church suffered severe fire damage on July 29, 1940, but was quickly rebuilt, the rededication ceremony being held on March 30, 1941. The Unitarian Church had last burned in 1875, and would burn again in the 1960s; but on both occasions the structure was swiftly rebuilt.

The only new organized religious group in Harvard since 1821 had been the Roman Catholic church. Before 1915 Roman Catholics in Harvard had attended Mass in Ayer, or even in Fitchburg. In 1915 a Catholic parish was established in Lancaster; Harvard became a mission of that church, and until 1926 Mass was said in the Harvard town hall. In 1925 construction of the present St. Theresa's Church was begun; the first Mass was said on May 30, 1926, and the building was dedicated on the following August 22. The name honored the 1925 canonization of St. Theresa; Harvard's was the first church in the Springfield diocese to take that name.

Harvard continued as a mission of Lancaster until 1950, when at the instigation of Bishop John Wright all small communities in such a position were constituted as independent parishes. In 1956 the rectory was built on land adjoining the church grounds.

Although Roman Catholics had lived in Harvard before 1915, the principal impetus to the establishment of a separate congregation was the large influx around the turn of the century of immigrants from various Catholic countries in Europe, particularly Ireland. Because many of these newly arrived Catholics worked on the railroad, they were known as "B&M Catholics."

Just as the dissolution of Shadrach Ireland's group of disciples upon the death of the leader had proved advantageous to the early Shakers, so the demise of the Shaker community nearly 140 years later provided an opportunity to yet another visionary—Fiske Warren. He did not really need the additional stimulus, for Warren was a man of action who manufactured his own opportunities and had already been putting his theories into practice, in Harvard and elsewhere.

Fiske Warren was a successful businessman who had become a disciple of Henry George and his "single tax" doctrine, and was anxious to perform a living social experiment based on George's principles. Henry George had expanded on a single feature of many older economic theories—the hypothesis that income derived from land rental (as opposed to the rental of improvements or developments on that land) was unearned income, and could be taxed at a 100 percent rate without interfering with economic growth based on various uses of the land. George further held that the revenue derived from the 100 percent tax on land rentals would be sufficient to cover all governmental expenses, and that no other tax would be required—no income tax, or sales tax, or excise tax; there would be only the "single tax" on land rental income.

More orthodox economists expressed serious doubts about these theories, observing that land rental was not the only form of unearned income, and that those being taxed were not always those who could afford such a high rate of taxation. But unlike many other economic theories, the single tax idea was put to the test, although on a limited scale. The first single tax community was established near Mobile, Alabama in 1895. By 1933 there were sixteen such communities, or "enclaves," most in the United States, but one each in France, Germany, and Andorra. Of these sixteen, two were in Harvard.

Fiske Warren began acquiring land in Harvard in the years immediately after the turn of the century, and on June 9, 1909 the first rental contract on the single tax plan was drawn up—about one acre rented to Ellen Mongovin. This one acre became the nucleus of the single tax enclave of Tahanto, which grew slowly but steadily; by the late 1930s there were 818 acres leased in the same way. Most of the acreage was in the immediate vicinity of Bare Hill Pond, concentrated mainly on the southern and eastern shores. The grounds of the Roman Catholic church and the Girl Scout camp were also included in Tahanto.

The early activities of Fiske Warren in Harvard were not predicated on the slow dissolution of the Shaker community; but when that group finally decided to leave Harvard, Warren was ready to move in. He acquired much of the Shaker land which became part of the Tahanto enclave. A second enclave was established in 1921; the first land put under contract was a six-acre parcel in Ayer. Later leases covered land in the northeast corner of Harvard as well as in Ayer. By 1933 this second enclave, known as Shakerton, had grown to include 140 acres of leased land.

At the instigation of Fiske Warren the various enclaves banded together each year from 1921 to 1933 to issue an annual report on each of the enclaves and on the state of the single tax movement as a whole. In the last report, a crude estimate was made of the consequences of extending the single tax system over the whole of the United States. In 1933 a little more than eight square miles of this country's land was under the single tax plan; the report estimated that if the entire land area of the country yielded rental income at the same rate as these eight square miles, the total rental would be about $20 billion. The report then noted that the entire governmental budget for the country —federal, state, and local—was $15 billion for the preceding

Sheep Island in Bare Hill Pond was one of Fiske Warren's single-tax properties. Enjoying a summer day here are Lou Sawyer, Alice Sawyer Bigelow, Mr. and Mrs. G. L. Sawyer, Mrs. A. S. Bigelow, Ethel Fairbank, Mr. and Mrs. H. H. Gale, Mr. A. A. Sawyer, and Louise H. Gale. (Courtesy Harvard Historical Society)

Miss Clara Endicott Sears, left, at the unveiling ceremony of the statue of Pumunangwet at the Indian Museum in June 1931. With Miss Sears are David Buffalo Bear and Philip S. Sears, the sculptor. (Courtesy Fruitlands Museums)

year, indicating a $5 billion surplus under a single tax levy. These oversimplified calculations are open to many criticisms, but adherents to the principles of Henry George were understandably encouraged.

Fiske Warren emphasized a particular aspect of Henry George's system. He saw the single tax system as protecting the little man against the greediness of the large landowner and landlord, and against the stinginess of factory owners and other employers. Warren felt that as long as the little man had a lease of land under the single tax plan, he would always have the option of returning to the soil and making a living as a subsistence farmer. Thus he could influence the wages paid by the industrial and commercial employers.

One can argue with these theories, but it is difficult to see how they could apply to Tahanto or Shakerton in any case.

Most of the land, especially that around Bare Hill Pond, was leased by well-heeled college professors and other professionals for use as summer residences. Other leaseholders were St. Theresa's Church, the Girl Scout camp, and the New England Telephone and Telegraph Company. The single-taxers liked to end each annual report on each enclave with the statement "There is no unemployment in Tahanto," or "There is no unemployment in Shakerton." A quick glance at the list of leaseholders reveals that this situation does not prove the validity of Fiske Warren's special theories.

Warren died on February 1, 1938, and most of the driving energy behind the single tax communities in Harvard went with him. The leases were soon terminated or renegotiated on more traditional terms, and yet another utopian experiment in Harvard passed into history.

Clara Endicott Sears was born in 1862, the same year as Fiske Warren, and her years of greatest activity in Harvard were the same as his. But that is the extent of the similarity between these two influential persons.

Miss Sears was born into a wealthy and well-connected New England family, received a good education, and read widely. After traveling for some time, she settled in Harvard and devoted the remainder of her life to a number of humanitarian projects, centering especially on the recording and preservation of the history of Harvard and the Nashua River Valley. During the years when Fiske Warren was acquiring land for Tahanto and Shakerton, and also at about the time when the Army was purchasing land for Camp Devens, Miss Sears was buying up land in Harvard, mostly on Prospect Hill overlooking the Plum Tree Meadows and the hills to the west. She built her home, the Pergolas, near the crest of Prospect Hill; portions of this building were designed after a monastery she had seen in Venice, just before its destruction. She also acquired and restored the farmhouse in which Bronson Alcott had started Fruitlands; the building was opened as a museum in 1914. Within a few years an old Shaker house, which had been moved to a site near Fruitlands and restored, also was opened to the public. These two buildings formed the nucleus around which was built the present Fruitlands Museums. Later additions were the Indian Museum in 1929, the Tea Room in 1935, the Picture Gallery in 1940, and the Reception Center in 1973.

Miss Sears also wrote extensively, mostly about Harvard and the vicinity. Her principal works of nonfiction were *Bronson Alcott's Fruitlands* (1915), *Gleanings from Shaker Journals* (1916), and *The Great Pow-wow* (1934; the story of the Nashua River Valley in King Philip's War). She also wrote a few novels, of which two were set in Harvard—*The Bellringer* (1915) and *The Whispering Pines* (1930).

When Clara Endicott Sears died in 1960, the trustees of her estate decided to tear down the grandly designed but poorly constructed Pergolas. This may have been a scenic loss to the town, but Miss Sears's legacy of historical writings and artifacts will be of value to Harvard's citizens and visitors for years to come.

The great hurricane of September 21, 1938 was one of the more dramatic occurrences in New England in the twentieth century; the storm caused nearly $500,000 damage in Harvard, according to contemporary reports. Seventy-five cottages on the Clinton Shore of Bare Hill Pond were stranded for four days after the storm because more than a hundred huge pine trees had fallen across the road. Damage to the town's apple orchards, in particular, was extensive.

"The Still River road is lined with uprooted trees," a local newspaper reported. "The Still River oval beggars description— everything gone. The Unitarian Church received a fateful gust, breaking the front stained glass window. The Congregational Church lost both chimneys, much slate from the roof and broken windows. The town hall lost its chimney and weather vane."

11

MODERN HARVARD: GROWTH AND PLANNING

In the years after 1940, Harvard grappled for the first time with a new approach to town government: town planning. The need for thoughtful planning was precipitated by a set of circumstances that had occurred only once before, at the very beginning of the town's existence, when access to Harvard's land was first established and the town's population dramatically increased. Since World War II, the population of the town has again increased rapidly; and in 1940 townspeople had no experience in planning sound policies to deal with a larger, more diverse population. Innovation was in order.

Harvard's population had indeed grown rapidly in the years just before the American Revolution; it rose from its 1732 level of three or four hundred to 1,126 in 1765 and 1,315 in 1776. At that time overcrowding had been no problem; the land in 1732 had been distinctly underpopulated, and the population of 1776 was appropriate for a New England farming community. For the next 170 years Harvard's population changed very little, increasing slowly to a peak of 1,630 in 1850 and then declining just as slowly until, in the 1920s and 1930s, fewer than 1,000 people lived in town. During World War II Harvard's population began to increase, but in 1945 the townspeople numbered only 1,065. More people had lived in Harvard in 1765.

Since 1945 the town's population has been increasing rapidly; it surpassed the 1850 peak in 1955 and reached about 3,500 in 1975. The town could not avoid pressures and problems that had never existed before; questions of land use, services, and commercial needs presented themselves for the first time. The town's responses to such questions and the changes stimulated by rising population are the most prominent features of the postwar years.

Railroad service had been established in Harvard in the middle of the nineteenth century, with the expectation that the town would grow and prosper as a result. These hopes were soon disappointed, for the railroad only facilitated the movement of young people away from Harvard, accelerating the phenomenon noted by the Reverend George Fisher in his 1832 centennial sermon. The railroad, then, aggravated economic stagnation in Harvard in the latter part of the nineteenth century by contributing to a decline in population and industrial growth.

As automobiles became more common in the early decades of the twentieth century, people used the railroads less and less. In the mid-1940s all passenger service to Harvard Depot and Still River Depot was discontinued, not one hundred years after it had begun. The region was not left without a major transportation artery for long, though. Already in the late 1940s numerous proposals were being set forth for a major east–west highway, passing through Harvard, and connecting Boston with western Massachusetts. One of the proposed routes would have entered Harvard at the Boxborough line, run along Route 111, and then passed along the southern shore of Bare Hill Pond and continued on into Lancaster. This route encountered considerable opposition, and was soon discarded in favor of one cutting through the north part of town in what was once Stow Leg. This new highway, Route 2, was opened to traffic in 1950. Only one or two families were displaced by the highway, but a number of scenic locations were obliterated by its construction; among these was the site of the East Family of Shakers.

The availability of this easy channel of access from Harvard to Boston and other urban centers has had a number of contradictory economic and demographic effects on Harvard. On the one hand, more people with jobs in Boston and elsewhere were attracted to live in Harvard because of the new ease of commuting. On the other hand, the growth of certain services such as supermarkets, banks, and other retail stores, which might have been expected to accompany the increase in population, did not occur; the presence of Route 2 and other improved state highways made it as easy to drive some distance to shop as it was easy to commute to work.

A highway on a grander scale was put through Harvard in the late 1960s but on this occasion there was little opposition—at least not so much as there had been to the construction of Route 2. Route 495, a six-lane superhighway that is part of the nationwide Interstate Highway System, traversed a thinly populated, swampy section in the southeast corner of Harvard, some distance from the focus of community activity.

The demand for public services rose greatly after 1940, putting new strains on the town budget and on the town officials who were forced to decide which services were truly essential. The heaviest demands were made upon the school system; the fire department and the police department were also augmented, though, and a new town ambulance service was initiated. Recreation began to be a significant town service, with the establishment and maintenance of the town beach and eventually of four new tennis courts behind the Bromfield School.

In 1940, only two buildings in Harvard were used by the town's schoolchildren—the old Bromfield Academy building and the Brown Building across the street—and neither was very large. The accelerated immigration in Harvard in the late 1940s, combined with the postwar "baby boom," made the construction of new school buildings inevitable. A proposal for a new school was made in town meeting on March 3, 1952, but was voted down. The next year the same proposal passed, the demands on the existing facilities having risen appreciably in the intervening months. This new brick building (the first half of the structure behind the Brown Building) was ready for use by the fall of 1954, and was occupied by most of the lower grades and the industrial arts class.

This was only a beginning; obviously, as the new elementary school students passed on to higher grades, the junior high and high school facilities would also have to be expanded. Thus, there were three more major construction programs in the 1950s and 1960s—the second half of the elementary school, the high school, and finally the middle school, which was ready for occupancy in the fall of 1970. Nor is this the end. School enrollment continues to increase, the Brown Building is rapidly becoming obsolete, and various proposals for additions to the elementary school system remain under consideration.

The magnitude of the demands placed on the town by the expansion of the school system can best be grasped by a very crude analysis of the town's budget for fiscal 1975. Harvard's total expenses for that year were just over 3.2 million dollars, of which about 2.0 million dollars had to be appropriated by the town through local taxes. For the same period the amount that can be directly and unequivocally designated school expenses was just short of 1.6 million dollars, of which more than 1.3 million dollars had to be appropriated. In a period of rapidly expanding public services and ever-escalating town budgets, the school system absorbs almost exactly one-half of the town's annual expenditures, and about two-thirds of its appropriations.

Like the schools, the town's other services were also forced to expand in the postwar years. The police department grew from a part-time force of one officer in the 1930s to a 1976 force of five full-time officers aided by a number of special and temporary police. At the same time, crime became a significant problem in Harvard for the first time in the town's history. In 1973 there were 66 reported instances of breaking and entering, and 85 cases of vandalism were reported in 1974. Such crimes were virtually unheard of as few as ten years earlier.

The town's volunteer fire department, essentially unchanged for decades, was provided with a new fire station in a

This view of the Unitarian Church dates from about 1900; the building burned down in December 1964. (Courtesy Harvard Historical Society)

1974 vote; the new building, located just west of the town hall and the old fire station, is scheduled for completion in 1976. The town's first ambulance squad, comprised of about fifteen volunteers with extensive medical and emergency training, was established in 1971; its first ambulance, a used vehicle, was replaced by a new ambulance in 1975.

Like other Massachusetts towns, Harvard sent its citizens to participate in three major wars since 1940—World War II, the Korean conflict, and the war in Vietnam. And as in the past, the cross-currents of religion and politics that resulted led to controversy and change in the town. In the midst of the nationwide anti-Communist fervor of the 1950s, a radical group of conservative Catholics known as St. Benedict Center purchased the Willard estate in Still River; like the Shakers and the Fruitlands experimenters, their agricultural community sought to convert others to their political and religious convictions. In the 1960s, the dissent occasioned by the Vietnam war showed up in an ideological split in the Unitarian church; the growing differences

among the congregation would lead in the 1970s to the formation of a new Unitarian group, the Nashoba Fellowship.

While the population of Harvard has tripled since the 1940s,
its business community has struggled and, in some cases, passed
away. Kerley, Reed and Bryant—the general store—passed in
the 1950s into the hands of David Reed, who was Reuben Reed's
son, and Edward Pieters. But the trend towards shopping out of
town at large regional shopping centers with modern supermarkets sounded the death-knell for general stores in small towns
across the country, and by the mid-1960s Harvard's had closed
its doors. Other small shops came and went: Bigelow's meat
market is gone, as is the small market in Still River; Carlson's
stand on Ayer Road is, in the 1970s, the only in-town source of
groceries and fresh produce. The general store building stood
vacant for several years before being converted into the Clothes
Corner, which sells women's garments. One restaurant and ice
cream stand survives in Harvard, but the fact that the town is
"dry"—no commercial establishment may sell or serve liquor—
makes the restaurant business even more precarious than it is
under more favorable conditions.

Commercial agriculture remains the largest industry in
town, but has steadily declined since World War II. There are, in
the mid-1970s, just three large applegrowers in Harvard—the
Carlson family, William Hermann, and Joseph Gringeri, who
bought the Doe brothers' orchards and has combined that operation with a successful cold-storage and trucking enterprise.
Dairying has faded even more rapidly; only two dairy farms
remain in town—those of the Watt brothers and St. Benedict
Center, both in Still River. There is also one beef cattle operation, the Websters' Whitney Lane Farms. Harvard's goat farm,
on Lancaster County Road, is a dying institution and, in 1976, is
about to be sold for back taxes.

Harvard's zoning (discussed in more detail in the next
section of this chapter) had designated Ayer Road north of
Route 2 as the town's principal commercial district. Charles
Eliot's 1970 study, *Planning for Harvard, Massachusetts*,
recommended, in an effort to avoid unattractive "strip" development, that business uses be "grouped" in this district, with

shopping uses in the southern portion and general service uses to the north. A site adjacent to the Route 2 interchange was suggested for a possible future shopping center under this plan, but before the grouping scheme could be put to a town meeting vote, Pandiscio Developers, backed by the Fitchburg Savings Bank, presented a plan for a shopping center at the northwest corner of Ayer and Old Mill Roads—in the area Eliot's "Master Plan" had suggested for general service uses. Construction on the Pandiscio project began in 1974, but problems plagued the development from the beginning, and after two years only a branch office of the bank had opened at the site.

One local industry does seem to have thrived in this uncertain economic climate: the real estate business. As property values skyrocketed in the postwar decades and more and more newcomers poured into town, competition among realtors became intense. In 1976, no fewer than nine real estate offices were operating in Harvard.

For two centuries before the Second World War, Harvard's land area had been divided into a number of modestly proportioned farms, usually owned and operated by the families who lived on the land. But the postwar influx brought to Harvard large numbers of newcomers who were not farmers. Many were professionals—educators, doctors, engineers, lawyers, and the like—who had retired or who wished to live in the countryside while working in or near Boston. By 1968, about 70 percent of the town's work force was employed in "white-collar" jobs, almost all of them located in other towns and cities. These new landbuyers certainly did not want to buy full-sized farms that would remain uncultivated; most of them were not interested in purchasing large tracts of land along with a house to live in. Soon there came to be more landbuyers than farms or houses available for sale; thus the pressures of the real estate market made Harvard a prime area for subdivision.

Another factor encouraged the trend toward subdivision of farmland into house lots. World War II heralded the end of widespread small-scale farming in Harvard and throughout Massachusetts. Nationwide changes in production and distribu-

This poster exemplifies the fears of many who pressed for zoning bylaws in the 1940s. (Courtesy Harvard Historical Society)

tion of agricultural products were making the small farm a less profitable economic venture. Rising property taxes exacerbated the problems of the small-scale agriculturalist, as the value of the land surpassed the purchasing power of prospective farmers. More and more farming families abandoned their agricultural activities, taking jobs in the burgeoning industrial areas around Harvard. The changing modes of production freed a great deal of land in Harvard for purchase by those who wanted smaller tracts on which to build new homes.

The largest residential subdivision that has been established in Harvard so far is the "Shaker Hills" development west and north of the Shakers' Holy Hill of Zion. Other areas which have seen relatively intensive residential development are the northwestern slope of Oak Hill between Littleton and Old Littleton Roads (Park Lane), the western slope of Bare Hill south of West Bare Hill Road (Woodside Road), and the former Westcott orchards and the area known as Enchanted Meadow on East Bare Hill.

Many Harvard residents saw in the increased tendency toward subdivision and denser residential usage of the town's land an undesirable deterioration of a typical small New England town. Elements of the town's topography and appearance that had remained unchanged for generations were disappearing, and a conservative reaction developed among those who wanted to preserve what they saw as the true character of Harvard. A curious aspect of this movement has been that relative newcomers to Harvard—the first people to change the demography of the town—have joined in an active and vocal alliance with residents who have lived here for many years. It has not been so much a desire for deliberate and beneficial growth that has dominated the town's planning, as a reaction against any growth that would fundamentally alter the structure of the town.

Early proposals for zoning bylaws were the first attempts to control changing patterns of land usage. Zoning bylaws were suggested in the late 1930s and throughout the 1940s, but not until 1951 was the first such bylaw approved by Harvard's voters. The long discussion that preceded enactment of this rudimentary "Protective Bylaw" attests to the importance of this step toward thorough town planning. A planning board was established in 1952 and guided the town's gradual revision and elaboration of its zoning; the Protective Bylaw was amended in 1953, 1956, 1958, 1963, and in virtually every year since then. The planning board adopted subdivision control regulations in 1954, updating them in 1965 and 1969.

The 1975 zoning bylaw sets forth eighteen distinct purposes for the numerous restrictions and regulations contained therein. Among these purposes are "to preserve and increase the amenities of the town," "to prevent overcrowding of the land," and "to conserve natural conditions and open spaces." These professed purposes, and many of the remaining fifteen, express the desire of the majority who approved the various bylaws to limit change in the town's physical constitution—to prevent the town from becoming choked with ugly commercial developments and traffic, or turning into a densely settled "bedroom suburb" comprised mainly of commuters.

The bylaw defines seven different types of land-use districts within the town: AR (agricultural-residential), B (limited business), C (commercial), I (industrial), MR (multiple residence), W (wetlands), and WFH (wetlands–flood hazard); it goes on to strictly delineate the kinds of activities which may be carried on and the kinds of structures which may be built in each district. Two well-known regulations peculiar to Harvard are the limitation of commercial and industrial enterprises to twelve employees, and the requirement that building lots contain at least one and a half acres of land. The first of these restrictions prevents the development of an industrial park of the type common in nearby towns, avoiding the possibility of extreme pollution and helping to minimize traffic on town roads. The second regulation, along with others, insures that houses in this residential town are well-spaced and, incidentally, expensive. Other regulations take advantage of Harvard's natural physical limitations toward similar ends; development of many parts of Harvard for high-density residential purposes is limited, for example, by the requirements of the board of health for adequate sewage facilities—requirements that because of the town's soil conditions are often prohibitive.

In July 1965 the planning board retained the services of Charles W. Eliot, a planning consultant, for the purpose of preparing a comprehensive "master plan" for Harvard. This plan, completed in March 1970, includes detailed information on the town's natural features, including topography, soil characteristics, and water supply; on existing land uses and development patterns; and on the various regional influences on the community. Eliot's findings and recommendations have formed the basis for most of the planning board's zoning refinements since 1970.

Part of the preparation for the Master Plan included the distribution of a questionnaire to the entire town; residents were asked for details of their homes, families, and businesses, and for their views on the most appropriate kinds of development for the town. Seventy-five percent of the households responded to the questionnaire, and the overwhelming majority expressed the desire to keep the town the way it was. "They would like to 'stop the clock,' " wrote Eliot, summarizing the results of the survey, "and 'close and bar the doors' to 'keep the population down.' Even some of the recent 'newcomers' say that since they chose to settle in Harvard because the town is 'small and friendly,' they would like to find a way to prevent others from following their own example."

The answers to specific questions showed that majorities of the respondents favored conservation of wetlands, requirements for large building lots, additional shopping facilities near the town center, prohibition of apartment buildings, and efforts to attract light industry to Harvard—this last apparently out of a belief that new industry would help lower the local property tax rate.

One of the innovations recommended by the Master Plan was the establishment of "historic districts" to insure the protection of the character of Harvard's three "villages"—the center, the Shaker Village, and Still River Village. Accordingly, a historic district study commmittee was set up, and in 1972 the Shaker Village Historic District was established. The Harvard Common Historic District was approved by the town meeting the following year, and both districts have since been expanded to include the buildings of the South Shaker Family and the "Little Common." Changes in the physical appearance of buildings within these districts, or construction of new buildings, may be carried out only with the approval of Harvard's historical commission. Attempts have been made to bring parts of Still River Village under the control of the commission, but have thus far been unsuccessful.

Zoning and historic district regulations are alike in dealing for the most part with land which is privately owned, and which is developed and occupied for residential or commercial purposes. A third method of preserving the physical character of the town is the removal of certain lands from private ownership, thus eliminating any possibility of development or undesirable change. The principal vehicle for this operation is the conservation commission.

The conservation commission was established by a vote of the town in 1962, and in its early years its prime responsibility was the administration of the various lands described in the state's Wetlands Protection Act—mainly the swampy areas along the brooks and rivers in Harvard. The commission's responsibilities were broadened, though, in 1968, when the town conservation fund was established. The fund provided money for the purchase of parcels of real estate which the town meant to retain as "open space." Since the establishment of the fund, several such tracts have been purchased, and others have been donated to the town for conservation. Indeed, Harvard spent enough money on land for conservation purposes to qualify for substantial reimbursements from the state and federal governments, and by 1975 had preserved far more open land than most Massachusetts communities. Although some townspeople complained over the years that an inordinate amount of money was being spent for this purpose, year after year the conservation fund was granted substantial appropriations at town meetings.

The town of Harvard faces a battery of land-use, conservation, and economic problems in the last quarter of the twentieth century. The sanitary landfill at the old Brookside cemetery site is nearing capacity, and the town began in 1975 to search for a new landfill site and at the same time explore alternatives for solid waste disposal. The problem of adequately disposing of sewage without polluting Harvard's water resources and thin, rocky soil looms ever larger as more and more dwellings, each with its own septic system, dot the landscape. The Bare Hill Pond Study Committee, an offshoot of the conservation commission, has undertaken detailed analyses of the biological processes that govern the health and water quality of the pond. The Nashua River, converted in an industrial age into an open sewer (mostly by industrial pollution upstream in Fitchburg and Leominster), has likewise begun to benefit from an increasing awareness of the importance of clean water resources. The Nashua River Watershed Association, organized in the late 1960s, has undertaken an ambitious program for establishing waste treatment facilities and preserving natural greenways along the entire length of the river.

The town water system, which serves only the public schools and the buildings in the immediate vicinity of the Common, is also nearing capacity use. This system was first established in the 1890s by the Hildreth brothers and then taken over by the town in 1940. Additional sources of water for the system are few and far between, and Harvard is faced with the prospect of a major pipeline construction project in order to connect a distant well with the present system—or perhaps even a water treatment plant for Bare Hill Pond. This problem, along with aforementioned needs for better solid waste and sewage disposal, could perhaps best be solved by the town's joining with one or more nearby communities for the pooling of resources. A number of regional planning agencies exist to help develop such solutions, but Harvard has thus far declined to join any of them.

The town has been under pressure from the state for a number of years to take part in another kind of regionalization —that of the public school system. The Bromfield School was, in 1975, the second smallest public high school in the state, and most of the surrounding towns had already formed regional school districts with one another. There is considerable local opposition to the trend towards regionalization, but the state makes it more difficult every year for Harvard to maintain its self-contained system.

The town economy, once agricultural and self-contained, has become almost totally dependent on outside jobs and outside shopping facilities. Harvard is now a "rurban" community, according to Charles Eliot's Master Plan, "in transition from an agricultural to a suburban residential town." The town's exports, Eliot wrote, "are no longer the products of the land and of water power, but it is the skills and services of the residents which are exported, as they commute outside the town boundaries to work. The land and water now serve as amenities for these residents. The residents value the 'rural' character of the town. However, as the town grows with new subdivisions overflowing from suburban towns closer to Boston, it will be subject to increasing pressure to provide new and additional local businesses and will require new tax revenue to expand and improve municipal facilities and services."

As these pressures mount, many Harvard residents have come to question to wisdom of the town's present zoning structure. Unquestionably, the Protective Bylaw has retarded commercial and industrial development while encouraging the construction of expensive houses on large, wooded lots. The town has thus become more and more a rural residential enclave for the wealthy, who in turn become more and more interested in keeping out commercialism and "the riff-raff." In many cases, this has meant that young people—particularly the children of old-time residents—are forced to leave the community, unable to find local employment and priced out of the Harvard real estate market. The destructive effects of this trend on a small and hitherto close-knit New England community have only begun to be seen, but will undoubtedly constitute one of the critical issues in determining the future direction of the town.

§ St. Benedict Center

Overlooking the most spectacular view in Harvard, in the rolling farmland of Still River, is set a pastoral scene reminiscent of many in medieval Europe. There, at St. Benedict Center, the Slaves of the Immaculate Heart of Mary live and work; their daily life shows little sign of a past encompassing a controversy with worldwide historic and religious consequences. St. Benedict's has lived peacefully in Harvard since 1958, following an orthodox Catholic religious routine whose philosophy includes many of the features of medieval monasticism; but it came to Harvard from an embattled and bitter existence in Cambridge and from the throes of the famous "Boston Heresy Case."

It is an extraordinarily complex case, fraught with emotion on every side. Its center is a basic disagreement between Father Leonard Feeney, head of St. Benedict's, and Catholic Church authorities on a theological issue—whether or not someone who is not a Catholic can go to heaven. In three decades of increasing liberalism, that doctrine has been interpreted less strictly by most of the Catholic hierarchy. Father Feeney's insistence on its strict interpretation—which resulted in his eventual apparent excommunication—is at the core of all St. Benedict's troubles, both with the Catholic Church and with members of the other faiths whom they excoriated.

Started in 1940 in Cambridge by Catherine Goddard Clarke as a Catholic study group for Harvard and Radcliffe students, the Center gained notoriety when Leonard Feeney's zealous proselytizing of the dogma *extra ecclesiam nulla salus*—outside the Catholic Church there is no salvation—became uncomfortably radical. In 1949 Feeney was dismissed from the Society of Jesus, and in 1953 a decree appeared in an official Vatican publication excommunicating him and suspending him from his priestly duties. Protesting that the decree was uncanonical and invalid, St. Benedict Center ignored the censures and gathered its forces for what it perceived as a battle for the truth.

For seven and a half years, in weekly demonstrations on the Boston Common, Leonard Feeney and his followers preached their doctrine to bitterly divided crowds. Their diatribes against the Jews especially—but also against Protestants and liberal Catholics—inflamed political and religious passions on all sides. Finally, in 1958, the Center drew into itself and retreated from the fray. With its move to the Willard estate in Still River, St. Benedict's began a new life—still focused on the *nulla salus* doctrine, and still including missionary work in the cities of America, but centered in a monastic, agricultural existence in Harvard.

All the lay members of the Center bound themselves by a solemn vow to their crusade. The married members renounced their relationships to their spouses; the men lived separately from the women, who were largely responsible for the communal care of the 39 children in the group. Calling themselves the Slaves of the Immaculate Heart of Mary, the few dozen brothers and nuns of St. Benedict's became a religious enclave startlingly similar in lifestyle to the Shakers Harvard had sheltered decades before.

A liturgical routine was established that followed closely the rule of such ancient monastic communities as the Benedictines. As well as the rites of holy office, classes and lectures in theology, philosophy, and Church history were attended daily. Meals were communal, but the brothers ate separately from the sisters and children. Days were long, starting well before 6 a.m. and with duties continuing until late in the evening. Well over 150 acres, much of it Haskell land to the south and Bigelow land to the north which the Center had purchased, provided ample room for the small herd of prize cattle the community acquired; soon they were able to supply all the milk and meat the Center needed, as well as sell some to the outside. And vigorous apostolic work in the outside world brought in a substantial income from the peddling of devotional literature published by the Center.

A small but rigorous school was established for the children of the community under the direction of carefully selected sisters. Although often the nuns were actually teaching their own children, the parental relationship was minimized. Children knew who their parents were, but they were allowed to visit with them only on special holidays such as feast days; in all other contexts they were under the moral, religious, and educational guidance of the appointed nuns. The brothers were actively discouraged from having anything to do with the upbringing of the children, even their own children. In fact, everything remotely having to do with the mixing of the sexes was tabu. The children were referred to as "little brothers and sisters," and from puberty on were strictly segregated in class and out. Over it all was the indomitable Sister Catherine Goddard Clarke, energetic, demanding, organized, whose powerful maternal presence balanced Father Feeney's more emotional, poetic nature and created an atmosphere that left few alternatives to obedience.

Though the community had assumed that the children at St. Benedict Center would eventually take the vows of their parents, it was inevitably that question that was to weaken and split the Center. In a bitterly fought court case, one of the brothers, Robert Colopy, renounced his membership in the community and sought to gain custody of his five young sons. Though the battle ended with the two oldest boys choosing to live at the Center, the seeds of discontent had been sown, and the future of the children became a major point of contention throughout the community. With Sister Catherine's death in 1968 and with Father Feeney's increasing age, severe strains developed that divided St. Benedict Center into two bitter factions, philosophically and psychologically opposed.

It was not surprising, then, when in 1971 another occurrence divided the groups—now living in separate houses at the Center—even more strongly. It was in that year that the Catholic hierarchy made overtures to St. Benedict's concerning the lifting of the censures that for two decades had hung over the community. Paradoxically, the very ecumenism that St. Benedict's condemned had led to a renewed tolerance in the Catholic Church for the radical right in its ranks.

The more liberal faction at the Center—St. Therese House, which had been more supportive of children who decided to leave the community—welcomed the offer of reconciliation, as long as it did not entail a repudiation of the *nulla salus* doctrine they had upheld for so long. But the other group, St. Anne House, was appalled. Cooperation with the lifting of censures, they claimed, would only recognize the validity of the original reason for the censures. As the Church was not willing to formally settle the doctrinal controversy, St. Anne House saw the issue in terms of hierarchical heresy; reconciliation, to them, would be betrayal.

On November 22, 1972, the Catholic Church removed from Leonard Feeney "any censures he may have incurred," requiring of the failing old man nothing more than that he profess the credo in which he had always believed. A little more than a year later, the majority group at St. Benedict's also professed their faith in front of the diocesan bishop, and were reconciled with the Church. Though St. Therese House insisted that they would continue to preach the *nulla salus* doctrine, their reinstatement was to irreparably widen the philosophical and psychological rift between the two factions at the Center.

In 1976, the two groups still face a tangle of legal problems in addition to their personal animosities. Though legally St. Benedict Center is one community, it functions as two—in separate living quarters, with separate agricultural and educational concerns, and retaining separate legal counsel. Neither group will give up the appellation "St. Benedict Center," causing confusion when both peddle their apostolic literature around the country. Ironically, the aged Father Feeney still presides over both groups, though each has its own *de facto* leadership. But it is a split with many deep-rooted causes, and one that more than likely will never be repaired.

—Kathleen Cushman

CONCLUSION

Having completed this brief survey of the history of Harvard, I do not intend to offer any predictions or speculations on the future course of that history. I would, rather, like to convey to the reader the most important impression that I have gained from this study of the directions of a town.

When Harvard was founded in 1732, the town was an extremely close-knit community of a little more than three hundred persons. There was only one church, and it transacted its affairs in the same building used for town business. Indeed the town meeting and church meeting can be viewed as two aspects of the same institution—the entire populace of the town acting as one organic, unified entity to direct all aspects of life in the town.

As Harvard evolved, this tightly unified structure was broken down into less integrated components. Other churches were founded, and finally, in 1820, the church was formally severed from the town. Communal aspects of other town activities disappeared or diminished—construction projects were let out to contract, rather than being done by all-volunteer labor; highway work was performed by hired laborers instead of by all landholders in town. These examples could be multiplied endlessly, but they all point in one direction; nearly every change in

Harvard's institutions and ways of life, whether these changes be termed progressive or regressive, can be seen as a movement away from the unified communal life of 1732.

At this point many will object that Harvard in 1976 still displays considerable community spirit, that the town meeting still works, and that volunteer workers can still be found for many projects. This point of view I believe to be correct, and I believe also that it leads to a conclusion not generally appreciated. The principles of communal living and communal thinking dominated and pervaded pre-Revolutionary Harvard—and other New England towns—to an extent which we of the twentieth century can hardly imagine.

Certainly everyone is aware that other towns have lost more of this spirit than has Harvard. Why is this? I can think of two reasons. The first is a simple appreciation of the positive values of communal cooperation, and an active effort to maintain these values, and at the same time resist the forces that would change and diminish those values. The second reason is more accidental; Harvard's topographical situation has allowed the town to avoid many of the economic and demographic pressures that have overcome other towns that were just as determined to retain the old communal principles. The town could not support exhaustive agriculturization, and there was not sufficient water power to attract the burgeoning industries of the mid–nineteenth century. The railroad, which was expected to attract people and business to Harvard, instead increased the drain on the town's human and economic resources. The generally poor condition of the town's soil has discouraged subdivision and residential development in the twentieth century.

This then is the one overarching concept that I have derived from my study of the town's records and activities. Harvard is not as integrated a community as it was two and a half centuries ago; but Harvard is still very much a community, more so than many other towns in the same part of Massachusetts. This is the greatest legacy that the present citizens of Harvard have received from those who have gone before—a legacy that should be in the mind of every Harvard citizen when considering and debating the directions the town will take in the years to come.

FIRST FAMILIES OF HARVARD

The following compilation of family data is not meant to be a thorough genealogical discussion of early families in Harvard. Instead, an attempt has been made to determine exactly which persons were residing in Harvard on June 29, 1732, the day of the town's incorporation. Thus this list may be considered a dummy census of Harvard on that date.

I have done some original research in court and town records, but for the most part I have relied on printed genealogies. In most families there are a few children whose history after birth cannot be traced; I have not included those children in this list. Hence this compilation provides a minimum population for the town in mid-1732. Certainly some of these children, especially the females, lived to have families, and have descendants living today. I apologize if I have omitted anyone's ancestor in this way. This minimum number can be increased in other ways—a family or two has no doubt been missed; adult but unmarried relatives of heads of families have not been diligently searched for; and the dozen or so Negro slaves must be taken into account.

The number in brackets at the end of each entry is the total of persons in that family alive on June 29, 1732. These numbers add up to a minimum population of 296. This may be compared with Nourse's cruder estimate of not less than 325 souls for the same date. When the various categories of missed and neglected persons are taken into account, this figure of 325 will be easily matched, and probably exceeded, but not by much.

A more detailed and documented genealogical treatment of these families has been prepared in typescript, and copies may be consulted at the Harvard Public Library, the Harvard Historical Society, and the New England Historic Genealogical Society in Boston.

1. Benjamin 3 (Joshua 2, James 1) Atherton, b. ca. 1700. Unmarried in 1732; later moved to Billerica, married, and died in 1739. [1]

2. James 3 (James 2, James 1) Atherton, b. 27 Feb 1685, m. Sarah. Children: Simon, bap. 1708; Amos, bap. 1708; John, bap. 15 Jan 1710; Abigail, bap. 27 Jul 1712; Sarah, bap. 27 Jun 1714; James, bap. 6 May 1716; Submit, bap. 7 Feb 1725; Prudence, bap. 25 Jun 1727. (Two other children probably died young.) [10]

3. John 3 (Joshua 2, James 1) Atherton, b. Jan 1702, m. Phebe Wright. Children: Phebe, b. 7 Feb 1731. (Nine children born later.) [3]

4. Joseph 3 (Joshua 2, James 1) Atherton, b. 1692, m. Hannah Rogers. Children: Oliver, b. 1 Aug 1721; Mary, b. 8 Mar 1722; Joseph, b. ca. 1728; Elizabeth, b. 7 Sep 1729; Hannah, b. 13 May 1731. (One child died before 1732, and one child born later.) [7]

5. Peter 3 (Joshua 2, James 1) Atherton, b. 12 Apr 1705, m. Experience Wright. Children: Experience, b. 13 Feb 1729; Azubah, b. 23 Dec 1730. (Twelve children born later.) [4]

6. John 2 (Richard 1) Burk, b. ca. 1670, m. Rebecca. (Seven children, all married or dead before 1732.) [2]

7. John 3 (John 2, Richard 1) Burk, b. 16 Apr 1704, m. Elizabeth Nutting. Children: James, b. 19 Jun 1727; William, b. 1 Feb 1729; Sarah, b. 26 Jun 1731. (Three children born later.) [5]

8. Joshua 4 (Isaac 3, Caleb 2, Richard 1) Church, b. 4 Mar 1708, m. Annis Johnson. Children: Joseph, b. 22 Jul 1729; Annes, b. 7 Jul 1731. (Seven children born later.) [4]

9. Jonathan 3 (Jonathan 2, William 1) Crouch, b. ca. 1695, m. Mary Whitney. Children: Jonathan, b. 1719; Mary, b. 1722; David, b. 1724; John, b. 1728. [6]

10. John 2 (Thomas 1) Daby, b. 26 Jan 1687, m. Hannah Buttrick. Children: Nahum, b. 23 Feb 1713; Simon, b. 27 Feb 1714; Joseph, b. 15 Dec 1716; Hannah, b. 20 Jan 1720; Mary, b. 24 Oct 1722. [7]

11. Eleazer 4 (Ebenezer 3, Simon 2, Dolor 1) Davis, b. 4 Mar 1703, m. Mary Perham. Children: Eleazer, b. 25 Sep 1730. (Six children born later.) [3]

12. John 4 (John 3, Samuel 2, Barnabas 1) Davis, b. 6 May 1698, m. Rebeckah Burt. Children: John, b. 10 Nov 1725; Zebudah, b. 11 Apr 1728; Rebecca, b. 29 Oct 1729. (Four children born later.) [5]

13. Joseph 4 (Jabez 3, Jonas 2, Jonathan 1) Fairbank, b. 1693, m. Mary Brown. Children: Phineas, b. 8 Apr 1719; Joseph, b. 4 Nov 1722; Cyrus, b. 23 May 1726; Mary, b. 19 Jan 1729; Lydia, b. 16 Aug 1731. (Two children died young before 1732, and three children born later.) [7]

14. Ephraim 3 (Jonathan 2, Matthias 1) Farnsworth, b. 2 Jan 1703, m. Deborah Beaman. Children: Deborah, b. 17 Sep 1727. (One more child born in 1734; Ephraim died in 1737.) [3]

15. Jonathan 2 (Matthias 1) Farnsworth, b. 1 Jun 1675, m. Ruth Shattuck. Children: Nathaniel, b. 1 Sep 1711; Hannah, b. 10 Aug 1716; Simeon, b. 12 Jul 1718; Susanna, b. 28 Apr 1720; Silas, b. 30 May 1723; John, b. 25 Apr 1725. (Seven others married or died before 1732.) [8]

16. Jonathan 3 (Jonathan 2, Matthias 1) Farnsworth, b. 27 Mar 1701, m. Mary Burt. Children: Mary, b. 18 Jun 1726; Jonathan, b. 22 Nov 1727; Betty, b. 13 Oct 1729; Joseph, b. 1732. (Five children born later.) [6]

17. Phineas 3 (Jonathan 2, Matthias 1) Farnsworth, b. 15 Sep 1707, m. Azubah Burt. Children: Azubah, b. 17 Jan 1731. (Seven children born later.) [3]

18. Reuben 3 (Jonathan 2, Matthias 1) Farnsworth, b. 28 Apr 1705, m. Mary Holden. Children: Mary, b. 16 Sep 1731. (at least two children born later.) [3]

19. Robert 2 (John 1) Foskett, b. 4 Apr 1672, m. (1) Mercy Goodwin (2) Susanna Whitney. Children: Robert; Abigail. (Probably had several other children, but records are scanty on this family.) [4]

20. Jacob 4 (Isaac 3, Stephen 2, Stephen 1) Gates, b. ca. 1698, m.

Elizabeth Hapgood. Children: Isaac, b. 6 Aug 1729; Zaccheus, b. 26 Aug 1731. (One child died before 1732, and five children were born later.) [4]

21. Shadrach 3 (Nathaniel 2, Shadrach 1) Hapgood, b. 6 Nov 1704, m. Elizabeth Wetherbee. (Ten children born after 1732.) [2]

22. Uriah 4 (Oliver 3, Henry 2, Nicholas 1) Holt, b. 25 Jun 1710, m. Sarah Wright. Children: Sarah, b. 18 Mar 1728; Uriah, b. 7 Feb 1730. (One child died young, and four children were born later.) [4]

23. Ephraim 3 (James 2, Ralph 1) Houghton, b. ca. 1700, m. Sarah Sawyer. (Two children died young, and two were born later.) [2]

24. Henry 4 (Henry 3, John 2, John 1) Houghton, b. ca. 1704, m. Elizabeth Randall. Children: Asa, b. 28 Mar 1727. (Three children probably died young, and three children were born later.) [3]

25. Stephen 3 (Jonas 2, John 1) Houghton, m. Abigail. Children: Abigail, b. 14 Jan 1727; Ebenezer, b. 4 Jul 1728. [4]

26. Thomas 3 (James 2, Ralph 1) Houghton, b. 1696, m. Moriah Moore. Children: Hannah, b. 1729. (One child probably died young, and two were born later.) [3]

27. Joseph 2 (Nicholas 1) Hutchins, b. ca. 1680, m. Elizabeth Wilder. (No children.) [2]

28. Annis Johnson, widow of Josiah 3 (Thomas 2, John 1) Johnson. She later married Benjamin Robbins. Children: David, b. 20 Aug 1715; Mary, b. 10 Nov 1719; Isaac, b. 17 Jul 1724; Josiah, b. 5 Jun 1726. (One child married before 1732, and two probably died young.) [5]

29. John 3 (Edward 2, Michael 1) Martyn, b. 10 May 1706, m. Mary Marrett. Children: John, bap. 21 Jun 1730; Mary, bap. 2 Jul 1732. (Three children born later.) [4]

30. Samuel 4 (Thomas 3, Israel 2, Gabriel 1) Meade, bap. 3 Mar 1706, m. Dinah Burt. Children: Hannah, b. 10 Apr 1729; Rebecca, b. Dec 1730; Samuel, b. 18 Jun 1732. (Ten children born later.) [5]

31. John Nichols, b. ca. 1698, m. Mary Priest. Children: Mary; John, b. ca. 1724; Jonathan; Daniel, b. ca. 1731. (At least five children born later.) [5]

32. Gabriel 2 (John 1) Priest, b. ca. 1690, m. Abigail. Children: John, b. 21 Nov 1717; Gabriel, b. 17 Jun 1720; Jeremiah, b. 30 Apr 1722. [5]

33. John 2 (John 1) Priest, b. 1 Nov 1691, m. Anna Houghton. Children: Anna, bap. 1708; Mary, bap. 1708; Rachel, bap. 1713; Hepsibah, bap. 1716; Jonathan, bap. 1718; Maria, bap. 1721. (One child died before 1732.) [8]

34. Joseph 2 (John 1) Priest, b. ca. 1692, m. Mary. Children: Joseph, b. 28 Nov 1717; Benjamin, b. 23 Mar 1719; Mary, b. 23 Mar 1721; Susannah, b. 22 Mar 1723; Eleazer, b. 23 Aug 1726; Tabitha, b. 5 Nov 1728; Bathshebah, b. 1 Mar 1731. (Three children born later.) [9]

35. Jonathan 2 (Henry 1) Rand, b. 1699, m. Abigail Whitney. Children: Silas, b. 21 Apr 1725; Elizabeth, b. 18 Mar 1727. (Four children born later.) [4]

36. Eleazer 2 (George 1) Robbins, b. ca. 1685, m. Ruth Wheeler. Children: Jedediah, b. 24 Aug 1709; George, b. 9 Jul 1712; Eleazer, b. 18 Jul 1714; Ruth, b. 13 Feb 1716; Ephraim, b. 2 Dec 1718. [7]

37. Samuel 3 (John 2, John 1) Rogers, b. 1672, m. (1) Grace Rogers (2) Elizabeth Stearns. (All children married or dead before 1732.) [2]

38. Samuel 4 (Samuel 3, John 2, John 1) Rogers, b. 24 Sep 1696, m. Isabella Houghton. (Children born after 1732.) [2]

39. Caleb 2 (Thomas 1) Sawyer, b. 20 Apr 1659, m. Sarah Houghton. (Five children, all married before 1732.) [2]

40. John 3 (Caleb 2, Thomas 1) Sawyer, b. ca. 1688, d. 1731, m. Ruth. Children: Joseph, b. ca. 1712; Paul, b. ca. 1723; Damaris, b. 1 Apr 1725; Dinah, b. 16 Feb 1728. [5]

41. Jonathan 3 (Caleb 2, Thomas 1) Sawyer, b. ca. 1690, m. Elizabeth Wheelock. Children: Caleb, b. 1720; Manasseh, b. 1729. (Six other children died before 1732, or no further record.) [4]

42. Seth 3 (Caleb 2, Thomas 1) Sawyer, bap. 1708, m. Dinah Farrar. (Dinah died in 1727; Seth married later and had five children.) [1]

43. Simon 4 (Simon 3, Simon 2, Simon 1) Stone, b. 1 Aug 1686, m. Sarah. Children: Simon, b. 10 Sep 1714; Ephraim, b. 2 Jan 1716; Oliver, b. 20 Jan 1720; Sarah, b. 27 Jan 1722; Isaac, b. 17 Feb 1724; Hannah, b. 18 Apr 1726; Elias, b. 2 Apr 1728; Amos, b. 9 Sep 1729. (Two children born after 1732.) [10]

44. Israel 2 (John 1) Taylor. (Married and had a family after 1732.) [1]

45. Seth 4 (Joseph 3, Samuel 2, Richard 1) Walker, b. 12 Oct 1691, m. Eleanor Chandler. Children: Seth, b. ca. 1719; Samuel, b. 30 Oct 1721. (Three children probably died young; two born after 1732.) [4]

46. Ebenezer 2 (John 1) Warner, bap. 1698, d. 1723, m. Mercy. Children: Anna, bap. 8 Apr 1716; Rebecca, bap. 20 Jul 1718; Ebenezer, bap. 4 Jun 1721; Mercy, b. ca. 1723. (Two other children probably died young.) [5]

47. Samuel 2 (John 1) Warner, b. 10 May 1680, m. Hannah. Children: Nathan, bap. 1713; Joshua, bap. 1713; Sarah. (Three other children died young or no further record.) [5]

48. John 3 (John 2, John 1) Wetherbee, b. 26 Jun 1701, m. Elizabeth Whitney. Children: John, b. 28 Aug 1723; Catherine, b. 1 Nov 1730. (Two children died before 1732, and seven were born later.) [4]

49. Thomas 3 (Deliverance 2, Thomas 1) Wheeler, b. 24 Jun 1697, m. Elizabeth Gates. Children: Thomas, b. 30 Jun 1723. (Two other children probably died young, and two children born later.) [3]

50. James 4 (Josiah 3, Josiah 2, John 1) Whitcomb, b. 1 Nov 1704, m. Hannah Graves. Children: Mary, b. 4 Mar 1729; Lois, b. 3 May 1731. (Seven children born later.) [4]

51. Elijah 4 (Isaiah 3, Thomas 2, John 1) Whitney, b. 3 Apr 1707. (Married and had seven children after 1732.) [1]

52. Isaiah 4 (Isaiah 3, Thomas 2, John 1) Whitney, b. 1 Jun 1700,

m. Elizabeth Whitney. (Two children born after 1732.) [2]

53. John 4 (Moses 3, Richard 2, John 1) Whitney, b. ca. 1700, m. Rebecca Whitney. Children: John, b. 20 Mar 1725; Ezra, b. 24 Aug 1731. (Two children probably died young, and one born after 1732.) [4]

54. Jonas 4 (Moses 3, Richard 2, John 1) Whitney, b. 1 Feb 1699, m. (1) Dorcas Wood (2) Margaret Stratton. Children: Jonas, b. 2 Jul 1727; Ephraim, b. 19 Sep 1728; Timothy, b. 7 Feb 1729; Margaret, b. 22 Oct 1731. (Two children died before 1732, and three children born later.) [6]

55. Jonathan 4 (Richard 3, Richard 2, John 1) Whitney, b. 26 Feb 1699, m. Alice Willard. Children: Jonathan; Betsey; Simon, b. 20 Mar 1719; Caleb, b. 4 Oct 1729; Oliver, b. 22 Jul 1731. (One child probably died before 1732, and four born later.) [7]

56. Richard 4 (Richard 3, Richard 2, John 1) Whitney, b. 1694, m. Hannah Whitcomb. Children: Mary, b. 24 Nov 1715; Dorothy, b. 13 Apr 1718; Daniel, b. 13 Feb 1720; Hannah, b. 29 May 1723; Richard, b. 31 Jul 1725; Elizabeth, b. 23 Jul 1728; Josiah, b. 12 Oct 1731. (One child born later.) [9]

57. Abraham 4 (Henry 3, Henry 2, Simon 1) Willard, b. ca. 1699, d. 1731, m. Mary Sawyer. Children: Abraham, bap. 5 Jun 1726; David, b. 20 Dec 1727; Mary, bap. 19 Apr 1730. [4]

58. Henry 4 (Henry 3, Henry 2, Simon 1) Willard, b. ca. 1703, m. Abigail Fairbank. Children: Henry, b. 11 May 1727; Abigail, b. 26 Sep 1728; Annis, b. 20 Jun 1730; Thomas, b. 11 May 1732. (Seven children born later.) [6]

59. Hezekiah 3 (Henry 2, Simon 1) Willard, b. ca. 1688, m. Anna Wilder. Children: Thomas, bap. 3 May 1713; Phinehas, b. 22 Oct 1714; Hezekiah, bap. 26 May 1717; Anna, bap. 3 Apr 1720; Mary, bap. 22 Dec 1722; Ephraim, b. 13 Oct 1726; Elizabeth, b. 28 Jan 1731. [9]

60. James 3 (Henry 2, Simon 1) Willard, b. ca. 1691, m. Hannah Houghton. Children: Isaac, bap. 27 Sep 1719; Asa, bap. 25 Jun 1721; Hannah, bap. 17 May 1724; Abigail, b. 17 Apr 1726; Experience, b. 2 Feb 1728. (One child probably died young.) [7]

61. John 3 (Henry 2, Simon 1) Willard, b. 3 Sep 1682, m. Anne Hill. Child: John, b. ca. 1715. [3]

62. Joseph 3 (Henry 2, Simon 1) Willard, b. ca. 1686, m. Elizabeth Tarbell. Children: William, bap. 24 May 1713; Sarah, bap. 22 May 1715; Tarbell, bap. 1 Nov 1719; Sybil, bap. 17 Feb 1723; Lemuel, b. 28 Jul 1725; Joseph, b. 17 May 1728; Amee, b. 25 Dec 1730. (One child died young, and one child born later.) [9]

63. John 2 (Walter 1) Wright, b. 10 Feb 1675, m. Mercy Wardwell. (Five children, all married or dead before 1732.) [2]

64. Samuel 3 (John 2, Walter 1) Wright, b. ca. 1704, m. Ruth. Children: Ruth, b. 5 Aug 1729; Mercy, b. 17 Mar 1731. (Seven children born later.) [4]

65. Thomas Wright, b. ca. 1705, m. Abigail Sawyer. Children: Thomas, b. 18 May 1730; Abigail, bap. 20 Feb 1732. (Five children born later.) [4]

INDEX